Ronald Reagan's

CONTRADICTIONARY

of the

AMERICAN
LANGUAGE

TOM PEYER

and

HART SEELY

Qp

QUINLAN PRESS
Boston

Published by Quinlan Press
131 Beverly Street
Boston, MA 02114

Cover design by Lawrence Curcio

Library of Congress Cataloging-in-Publication Data

Peyer, Tom, 1954-
  Ronald Reagan's contradictionary of the
American language.

  1. Reagan, Ronald—Language.   2.
Reagan, Ronald—Humor.
I. Seely, Hart, 1952-   II. Title.
E877.2.P48   1988   818'.5407   87-63618
ISBN 1-55770-056-7

Printed in the United States of America
February 1988

To Tom's mom and dad.

H.S.

To Hart's parents.

T.P.

The authors wish to thank the following people for their help and support: Steve Carlic, Jim Ehmann, Tom Marr, Tom Riker, Susan Tuohy, Janice Whitcraft and the gangs at the *Syracuse New Times* and Syracuse Newspapers.

Tom Peyer is a cartoonist for the weekly *Syracuse New-Times.* *Sideshow,* a collection of his political cartoons, was published in 1982.

Hart Seely is a reporter and columnist for the *Syracuse Herald-Journal.* He has won numerous writing awards, including the 1984 New York State Publishers Award for investigative reporting.

Foreword

"If thought corrupts language,
language can also corrupt thought."
George Orwell (1946)

"It's hard to tell where legend ends
and reality begins."
Ronald Reagan (1965)

In our lives, no American politician has used the English language more effectively than Ronald Reagan. From the "rescue mission" in Grenada to the "Peacekeeper" missile, the President has persistently cloaked reality within a cheery rhetoric. He has been one of America's most loved leaders.

Here are definitions of some words and phrases that the Great Communicator has used over the last thirty years. They come from news accounts of Reagan's statements as governor, candidate, author and President.

We hope this book sheds some light on the words and phrases that have composed Ronald Wilson Reagan.

And we offer it in the memory of collateral damage, everywhere.

Guide to the Use of this Contradictionary

I. American Words

All entries, including phrases, proper nouns and exclamations derive from public utterances and verbal spankings administered by the President, the First Lady and their handlers. No Democrat or liberal funny business is allowed in the *American* language.

Which is as it should be.

Each entry has been invoked on at least one occasion to strengthen American traditions and combat communism, at home and abroad.

Some words offer dual meanings. That makes them better than entries with only one definition. In such cases, the *Contradictionary* salutes the improvements in these words by displaying their multiple uses.

Unfortunately, not all *American* words could be collected in this volume. New entries are being composed each day by office-seekers — of all parties — who have dedicated themselves to the continuing battle against clarity and information.

Contradictionary

II. Pronunciations

Each entry offers a phonetic spelling for proper pronunciation.

Example: **I·ran·scam** (*wa' ter gāt*)

Through this pronunciation, *Contradictionary* users can explain the meanings of words to people who cannot read or write. These people are known to be especially dependent upon the *American language.*

Key to Pronunciations

a	Cap, nap, CRACK!, klan	**o**	Mommy, bomb, Ollie
ā	Haig, Casey, crazy, shame	**ō**	gold, old, Rambo
ä	Watt, god, gosh	**ô**	Bork, dork
e	Helms, Wedtech, Kemp, stench	**o͞o**	voodoo, doomsday, nuke
ē	Meese, grease, sleaze	**oo**	crooks, bloodbath
ee	queer, fear, rear, jeer	**oi**	Poindexter, coin
i	Nixon, Bitburg, Gipper, wimp	**ou**	Shout down
ī	Iran, Mines, might, right	**u**	Bush, slush fund

III. Etymology

After each phonetic spelling, the year that the entry was defined is listed.

All *American* definitions and quotations derive from the President, who was elected and re-elected for this purpose.

If the First Lady or a handler has redefined the word, she or he is credited as the *contributor.*

2

Example: **Kick a lit · tle ass** (hah), v., 1984. Win a debate with a girl. [*Contributed by Vice President George H. W. Bush*]

Exception: If the handler is former Secretary of State Alexander Haig, each definitionalization is contributionalized according to regular grammaticalization of dictionaryalysis.

IV. Definition

This is what the word means, according to Presidential policies.

Example: **Res · cue mis · sion** (wôr), n., 1983. *The invasion of a small country to halt the spread of communism.*

With these definitions, Americans can better appreciate their government. For example, in 1983 reporters asked:
"Mr. President, would you invade Grenada?"
The answer was "no."
Had reporters studied a *Contradictionary*, their proper question would have been:
"Mr. President, would you send *peacekeepers* on a *rescue mission* into an *outlaw state* run by *leftist thugs* orchestrated by the *evil empire*?"
Obviously, the answer would have been different.

V. Cross-references

To offer readers a better understanding of the *American* language, many entries are cross-referenced with other words.

3

Contradictionary

Example: **Free·dom fight·ers** (kon′traz), n., 1986. Patriots everywhere who combat communism, no matter what it takes. [*See NUNS, SCHOOL BUSES*]

These references supplement one's ability to refute Democrat or liberal funny business.

VI. **Illustrations**

As a special service to *Contradictionary* users, several entries are further illustrated through the use of illustrations. These pictures were prepared by scholars, linguists, social scientists and bearded artists who were paid to approximate the President's point of view.

Unfortunately, when employing pointy-headed college professors and professional students who think the world owes them a living, one must expect them to undermine the impartial text with their own ignorant opinions.

If this has happened, we apologize.

A

Aaaa (uhh), exclamation, 1981–88. A thoughtful sound occasionally made by the President.

Ac·id rain (ded lāks), n., 1981–88. Canada's polluted precipitation, which America would remedy if only we could figure out where it comes from.

Af·fir·ma·tive ac·tion (no ak′shun), n., 1982. Job discrimination against non-underprivileged people.

Aides (gīz), n., 1966–88. Men the President tries to obey.

AIDS (godz rē venj′), n., 1984–88. A disease that decent people don't have to fear. [See ROY COHN]

Air strike (our rē venj′), n., 1986. A tool of American diplomacy that features the bombing of civilians. [See COLLATERAL DAMAGE]

See **Aides**

AM · CIT (vōt' er), abbreviation, 1986. An *AM*erican *CIT*izen, the most valuable person in the world. "One 707 [plane] with 300 TOWs [missiles] = 1 *AMCIT.*" [Contributed by Lieutenant Colonel Oliver L. North] [See RANSOM]

A · mer · i · ca (a mer' i ka), n., 1983. "God's chosen place." [Contributed by Secretary of the Interior James G. Watt]

A · mer · i · can Civ · il Lib · er · ties Un · ion (push' ē loi' erz), n., 1981. The "criminals' lobby." [Contributed by White House Counsellor Edwin Meese III]

A · mer · i · can farm · ers (tuf luk), n., 1982. "Miracle workers of the Western World." [See AUCTIONS, BANKRUPTCY, FARM CRISIS, SUICIDES]

A · mer · i · ca's cru · sade (hīp), n., 1986. A nationwide response to the First Lady's courageous personal war against the drug crack. "Starting today, Nancy's crusade . . . becomes *America's crusade.*" [See HYSTERIA]

A · mer · i · ca's lob · by · ist (pak' man), n., 1984. The President.

A · mer · i · ka (rā' tingz di zas' ter), n., 1986. A stunning TV miniseries that realistically depicts what will happen if America chickens out of World War III. [See HYSTERIA]

An · ti · war pro · tes · tors (sis' ēz), n., 1965-70. "Cowardly little fascist bands" of "jack-booted young monsters" who want to turn colleges into "staging grounds for insurrection." The only question is "whether what they want is victory for North Vietnam or peace." [See COLLEGE STUDENTS]

Ap · pear · ance prob · lem (skan′ dl), n., 1985. The absurd suggestion of impropriety surrounding Attorney General Edwin Meese III's acceptance of an interest-free loan from a friend who later just happened to get a federal job. [See SLEAZE FACTOR]

A · rabs (teks′ e kō), n., 1987. "Sand niggers," according to White House aides. [Contributed by former Secretary of Education Terrel H. Bell]

Are you bet · ter off to · day? (dōnt ask!), exclamation, 1980. The proper concern of modern voters: not what you can do for your country, but what your country has done for you, lately.

Ar · i · as Peace Plan, the (thret tōō wôr), n., 1987. A shady-looking deal proposed by one of those two-bit leaders down there that lets the Nicaraguans off the hook and jeopardizes America's freedom fighters. [See NOBEL PEACE PRIZE]

Ar · ma · ged · don (juj′ ment dā), n., 1. 1981. The end of the world, which could come any minute now, at the hands of America's God, who is fed up with abortion, the lack of a death penalty and being kicked out of classrooms. [See FOOTBALL] 2. 1981. The imminent apocalypse that excuses America from preserving her natural resources. [Contributed by Secretary of the Interior James G. Watt]

Arms build · up (dē fens′ pakts), n., 1983. Giving birth to new nuclear weapons in order to ward off slavery.

Arms con · trol (dē fens′ kuts), n., 1. 1976–80. A myth about trust and world harmony promoted by liberals and Democrats that threatens meaningful peace. [See TOTALITARIANISM] 2. 1981–86. A goal that can only be attained if America builds more bombs. 3. 1987–88. The President's greatest achievement.

Arms con · trol a · chieve · ment (shel gāmz), n., 1981–88. The art of deploying mid-range nuclear weapons in Europe at the beginning of an administration so that you can pull them out at the end.

Arms con · trol stra · te · gy (stäl), n., 1985. A grueling test of peacemaking endurance. "The one who loses is the one who gets tired first." [See NAP]

Arms for hos · tag · es deal (frē en′ tur prīz), n., 1. 1986. A policy the President didn't know about. [See DETACHED MANAGEMENT STYLE] 2. 1986. A policy conceived by the President. [See CLARIFICATION] 3. 1986. A policy the President didn't know about. [See PLAUSIBLE DENIABILITY]

Arms sum · mit (bul′ sesh un), n., 1987. A chance to dupe the Russians, lock up the next Nobel Prize and obtain peace from the First Lady.

Arms trans · fer (ran′ sum), n., 1986. The exchange of American weapons for American hostages. [See NEVER]

Arm wres · tle (dūk it out), v., 1984. To test a man's true Presidential mettle. After the President's debate with Democratic candidate Walter Mondale: "I'll challenge him to *arm wrestle* any time." [See MENTALLY ALERT]

Ash heap of his · tor · y (dust tōō dust), n., 1982. The ultimate destination of Marxism-Leninism. [See ARMAGEDDON]

Ass (buhhht), n., 1987. The part of Lieutenant Colonel Oliver L. North's anatomy that the President "loves." [Contributed by Mr. North] [See PARKLANE HOSIERY]

See **Average guy**

At cost (līk hel wē wil), adj., 1985. Cheap; without profit. When America's outer-space peace umbrella is in place, we will sell it to the Soviets *"at cost."* [See SURRENDER OR DIE]

Av · er · age guy, the (non vō′ ter), n., 1986. The common man, who loves his President. "All he knows is that the Russians wanted us to give up SDI, and Dutch Reagan said, 'Blankety-blank, no way.' That's the level it's on for *the average guy.*" [Contributed by White House Communications Director Patrick J. Buchanan] [See TRADITIONAL FAMILY]

See **Bork**

B

B-1 Bomb·er (rok'wel korp), n., 1981. An aircraft so vital to America's defense it must be built before being fully designed. [See FLYING EDSEL]

Back-chan·nel com·mu·ni·ca·tion (nō'bud ē telz mē nuh'thin), n., 1986. A conversation that excludes Secretary of State George P. Shultz. [Complained about by Mr. Shultz]

Bal·anced budg·et (fat chans), n., 1980. The only way to run a government: spending just what you take in. "We can do it. We must do it. And I intend that we will do it." [See DEFICIT]

Band-Aid so·lu·tion (prē ē lek'shun sum'it), n., 1984. Quick answers to complex problems. "*Band-aid solutions*" provide instant relief but no long-range cure. The President avoids them. [See AIR STRIKE, CRACK, DEFICIT, EVIL EMPIRE, IRANSCAM, MAD DOG, PATCO]

Bar·gain·ing chip (bom), n., 1983. A weapon that must be funded by Congress so it can be sacrificed in an arms control agreement, which won't come about because of the presence of that weapon. [See ARMS CONTROL STRATEGY]

Beau·ti·ful white peo·ple (rā' gun vōt' erz), n., 1980. Admirers of the First Lady at a GOP rally in Rosemont, Illinois. [Contributed by the First Lady]

Bech·tel Pow·er Corp. (sē ī ā), n., 1981. The U.S. State Department. [See W. KENNETH DAVIS, PHILLIP HABIB, GEORGE SHULTZ, CASPAR WEINBERGER]

Bed (zzz), n., 1966. A fine place to scare North Vietnamese leader Ho Chi Minh. "He should go to *bed* each night afraid that we might (use atomic bombs)." 2. 1986. A fine place to scare Libyan leader Moammar Gaddaffi. "We would just as soon have Mr. Gaddaffi go to *bed* every night wondering what we might do." [See AIR STRIKE] 3. 1987. A fine place to scare Iranians. "I think it's far better if the Iranians go to *bed* every night wondering what we might do." [See AIR STRIKE] 4. 1980–88. The Oval Office from 1 to 3 P.M. daily.

Bel·ly but·ton (maks' wel smart), n., 1987. Slang. A Swiss bank account named for a joke about Lieutenant Colonel Oliver L. North. Merchant Albert Hakim refuses to tell the joke in public. [See "DO YOU HAVE ANY MORE OF THOSE PICKLES WITH THE BONES IN THEM?"]

Beer·y, Wal·lace (kold ham), n., 1981. The President's greatest disciplinary challenge to date. "Listen, I once made a movie with *Wallace Beery*. After that, nothing could distract me."

Belt·way blood-let·ting, a (wa' tur gāt tōō), n., 1986. The

14

Iranscam controversy, which nobody cares about outside Washington. [See OLLIEMANIA]

Bi · ble, The (trī umf uv pol' i tiks), 0–1987. 1. The book that "contains an answer to just about everything and every problem that confronts us." It calls upon America to stop being so chintzy on her armed forces. 2. An autographed gift sent to Iran, along with a chocolate cake and some colt revolvers, to prove America's sincereity in the swap of arms for AMCITs. [See GALATĪANS]

Big spend · ers (blēd' ing harts), n., 1982. Democrats and liberals in Congress who produced the national deficit, hold secret allegiance to the Soviet Union and drove prayer out of our classrooms. [See TOTALITARIANISM]

Bit · burg Cem · e · ter · y (for' est lawn), n., 1985. A final resting grounds in Germany for "young men [who were] victims of Nazism also, even though they were fighting in the German uniform." [See CLARIFICATION]

Bitch (nyah nyah nyah),n., 1984. A term for Democratic Vice Presidential candidate Geraldine Ferraro that Second Lady Mrs. George H. W. Bush cannot bring herself to utter: "A four-million-dollar — I can't say it, but it rhymes with 'rich'." [Contributed by Mrs. Bush] [See RUNT]

Bite the bul · let (starv), n., 1982. The gritty self-sacrifice encouraged of Americans due to a soggy economy. [See SOGGY ECONOMY]

Bit · ter bile in my throat (ralf), n., 1986. The sour aftertaste from vicious attacks by the leftist press just because the President tried to free America's hostages. [See RANSOM]

Black lead · ers (werz sam' ē dā vis?), n., 1985. Loudmouths we can do without. "They're reluctant to admit how much they've achieved, because it might reveal then that there's no longer a need for that particular organization, which would mean no longer a need for the job.''

Blink (wimp out), v., 1986. To cave in during an eyeball-to-eyeball duel with communism. The Soviets *"blinked."* The President will not *"blink."* [See ONE TOUGH SON OF A BITCH]

Blood (kash), n., 1986. Bodily fluid that each American should personally stockpile to avoid catching AIDS.

Blood bath (kent stāt), n., 1970. The inevitable clash between Soviet-backed hippy freaks and America's boys in blue. "If it takes a *blood bath*, let's get it over with." [See ARMAGEDDON]

Blue dye (tī′ dē bōl), n., 1987. A patriotic hue that, when flushed into government bathrooms, renders toilet water useless to federal junkies and dope mobsters who would love to dilute their urine samples. [See DIRECT OBSERVATION]

Blue·print for bond·age (taks hīk), n., 1984. The proposed economic policies of Democratic Presidential candidate Walter Mondale. [See TOTALITARIANISM]

Bob Jones U·ni·ver·si·ty (thrē kā ko′ lij), n., 1982. A top school where God-fearing youths learn the importance of choosing the right friends. Sadly, it does not receive federal tax-exempt status. [See SEPARATION OF RACES]

Bo·he·mi·an Grove (kamp′ fīr boiz), n., 1872–1988. A men's club for corporate and world leaders, including the President. Members gather to sing camping songs, speak candidly about women and short-sheet each other's beds. [See GEORGE BUSH, STEPHEN BECHTEL, WILLIAM HEARST, RICHARD NIXON, CASPAR WEINBERGER]

See **Bombing Russia**

Bol·and A·mend·ment, the (hoo cārs), n., 1986. A stupid bureaucratic regulation that endangers humanitarian aid to the Contras merely because Congress wasn't told about something. [See SLUSH FUND]

Bo·liv·i·a (doun ther), n., 1982. Any South American country. "Would you join me in a toast to President [Joao] Figueiredo, to the people of *Bolivia* — no, that's where I'm going — to the people of Brazil — and to the dream of democracy and peace here in the Western Hemisphere." Aides later informed the President he was headed for Bogota, Colombia, not *Bolivia*. [See CLARIFICATION].

Bomb·ing Rus·sia (har dē har), n., 1984. The funniest thing the President could think of before one weekly radio broadcast. "My fellow Americans, I am pleased to tell you today that I've signed legislation that will outlaw *Russia* forever. We begin *bombing* in five minutes." He later quipped that he had no plans to *bomb Russia* "in the next five minutes." [See ARMAGEDDON]

Bombs (dip lō′mu sē), n., 1983. Items whose "only value in possessing. . . is to make sure they can't be used." [See ARMS BUILDUP]

Bon·zo (meth′ud ak′ter), n., 1951. A chimpanzee who, in front of a camera and with the help of expert handlers, acted like something he wasn't. [See AIDES]

Bood·lers (mil′u tents), n., 1985. Black leaders who supported Democratic Presidential candidate Walter Mondale. [Contributed by White House Communications Director Patrick J. Buchanan]

Bor·ing (zzz), adj., 1984. Dreary, dull. The nature of White

House cabinet meetings, which explains why the President occasionally dozes off. [Contributed by former Deputy White House Chief of Staff Michael K. Deaver] [See DETACHED MANAGEMENT STYLE, CHURCH]

Bork, Rob·ert H. (jon berch), n., 1927–88. A man who will "go down in history as one of the finest Supreme Court Justices our nation ever had." [See ABORTION, CENSOR-SHIP, DEATH PENALTY, FORCED STERILIZATION, POLICE RAIDS, PRIVACY, POLL TAXES, TURNING BACK THE CLOCK, WIRETAPPING, SATURDAY NIGHT MASSACRE]

Born a·gain budg·et-bal·an·cers (band wag un), n., 1984. Democrats and liberals who, merely for political gain, condemn the $180 billion federal deficit. [See TOTALITARIANISM]

Bot·u·lism ep·i·dem·ic (tēē hēē), n., 1974. An act of divine justice that "it's just too bad we can't have" following the free-food giveaway to poor people by the family of Patty Hearst, as partial ransom for their daughter being kidnapped.

Brain·wash·ing (skōōl′ ing), v., 1984. Transforming American children into leftist thugs. The National Educators Association published a *"brainwashing"* guide for teachers that claimed that, a) racial discrimination exists in the United States and that, b) options exist "to resolve conflicts among nations by means other than nuclear war." [See DIPLOMACY]

Break·age (liv līk trash), n., 1981. The sad but inevitable destruction of White House china. "Now, *breakage* occurs, even in the White House. . . The truth of the matter is, at a state dinner, we can't set the table with dishes that match." [See GODDAMN BACK]

See **Breakage**

Broad in · ter · pre · ta · tion (skrap it), n., 1986. A more alert reading of the 1972 Anti-Ballistic Missile treaty that allows America to build a peace umbrella in outer space. [See CREATIVE AMBIGUITY]

Buck (dōnt wāk him), n., 1987. The final, all-encompassing responsibility that "stops" at the desk of America's National Security Advisor. [Contributed by Rear Admiral John M. Poindexter]

Budg · et · bust · er (bīz nō gunz), n., 1. 1981. A government program that throws good money after the environment, poor people or jobs. 2. 1983. A Democrat or liberal who favors nondefense spending. [See TOTALITARIANISM]

Bul · wark a · gainst ag · gres · sion (līk south af' ri kuh), n., 1981. Any country that hates Russians. [Contributionalized by Secretary of State Alexander M. Haig, Jr.]

Bum rap (y-y-yes deer), n., 1981. A reputation for uppitiness unfairly assigned the First Lady for merely wanting a set of new White House china. [See MOMMY, HACKLES]

Bunch of crap (put kāy'sē on em), n., 1987. Carping by Democrats and liberals about having to spend a little money so Americans don't live in fear of a Soviet invasion. [See TOTALITARIANISM]

Bu · reau · crat · ic boon · da · gle (rē portz' tōō rēd), n., 1983. The U. S. Department of Education.

Bu · reau · crat · ic sab · o · tage (lēks), n., 1981. Mean-spirited attempts by anonymous federal workers to harm crucial cutbacks in America's school lunch program. [See CATSUP]

See **Bush**.

Bush, George Her·bert Wal·ker (wotzisnām), n., 1. 1980. A prissy egghead from Maine whose wishy-washy beliefs are molded by the Eastern Liberal Establishment. [See VOODOO ECONOMICS] 2. 1981–83. America's presence at funerals and weddings. 3. 1984. A tough-talking Texan whose hard-line conservatism is as unquestioned as his masculinity. [See KICK A LITTLE ASS] 4. 1985–86. America's presence at funerals and weddings. 5. 1987–88. A tough-talking Texan whose hard-line conservatism is as unquestioned as his masculinity. [See WIMP FACTOR]

Bus·i·ness com·mu·ni·ty (bak′erz), n., 1983. "The primary constituents of this administration." [Contributed by former Environmental Protection Agency assistant administrator for toxic wastes Rita Lavelle]

See **Casey, William**

C

C·I·A (sē′crit guv′urn ment), n., 1947–88. [See EVERYWHERE]

C·I·A em·ploy·ees (has′en fus), n., 1982. "Heroes in a grim twilight struggle." [See CAR BOMBS, TECHNIQUES OF PERSUASION]

Car·ter, Jim·my (mis′ter pē′nut), n., 1924– . The thirty-ninth President of the United States. His administration caused present-day budget deficits, high unemployment, drug and alcohol abuse, the Soviet invasion of Afghanistan, the deterioration of family values, a weakened American military, the Panama Canal giveaway and the cancellation of "Little House on the Prairie."

Ca·sey, Wil·liam J. (god′fa ther), n., 1913–87. The former head of the Central Intelligence Agency and "one of the heroes of America's fight for freedom." [See ARMS TRANSFER,

25

Blind Trust, Contras, Covert Operation, Cowboys, De-bategate, Domestic Spying, El Salvador, Hasenfus, Iranscam, Marcos, Neutralizations, Nicaragua, Oliver North, Possibly Dead, Project Democracy, Sleaze Factor, Slush Fund, Swiss Bank Account, Taxicab Bomb, Techniques of Persuasion, Ultimate Covert Operation, White House Basement, White House Mole, Deathbed Confession]

Cas·u·al con·ver·sa·tions (houz thuh we′ther?), n., 1987. Frequent talks between Attorney General Edwin Meese III and several of the Iranscam conspirators. Nothing worth noting was said, ever! [Contributed by Mr. Meese] [See Memory]

Catch·ing the dick·ens (halllp!), v., 1987. Being verbally spanked because of Presidential policies. [Contributed by Vice President George H. W. Bush] [See Deep Doo-doo]

Cat·sup (kech′ up), n., 1981. A vegetable. If Americans had accepted this definition, supplied by federal budget nutritionists, taxpayers could have saved $300 million a year in school lunch programs. [See Gosh]

Cha·os (ev′ rē man for him self′), n., 1987. The state of White House operations following the public disclosure of arms transfers to Iran. [Contributed by The Tower Commission]

Char·ac·ter as·sas·sins (lē′ gul skol′ erz), n., 1984. Critics of attorney general appointee Edwin Meese III. [Contributed by Mr. Meese] [See Interest-free Loan]

Cheap shot (nōōōz), n., 1980. A smear attack by leftist reporters merely because the President happened to tell a rib-tickling joke. [See Polish Guy, Italian Guy]

Cheese sur·plus (let them ēt kāk), n., 1981. America's solution to hunger.

See **Catsup**

Chem·i·cal peo·ple (bumz), n., 1983. Drug users. [Contributed by the First Lady] [See MOMMY, NO, DOUGLAS GINSBURG]

Chi·na (skrōōo tī wan′), n., 1. "Red *China,*" 1979. A nation of such totalitarian infamy that to open diplomatic relations was to "cold-bloodedly betray a friend (Taiwan) for political expediency. The memory will not go away." [See MEMORY] 2. "So-called Communist *China,*" 1984. A nation of rich history and happy Asians who, since they hate Russia as much as we do, have a destiny of "going forward hand-in-hand" with America. 3. 1981–88. A breathtaking selection of dinnerware that, despite sad and inevitable breakage, delights all who dine with the First Family. [See BUM RAP]

Choke points for free·dom (gag), n., 1986. Sixteen places across the globe where Good is fighting Evil.

Church (zzz), n., 1981–88. A house of God that the President must avoid to save lives. "I represent too much of a threat to too many other people for me to be able to go (to *church*)." [See BORING]

Church·men (ping′ kōz), n., 1983. Agents of discord who want "to see Soviet influence in El Salvador improved." [Contributed by Secretary of State George P. Shultz]

Civ·il Rights Act (dōnt thā hav ē nuf′?), n., 1964. "A bad piece of legislation" full of "flaws and faults." [See SLAVERY]

Civ·il Rights lead·ers (not him), n., 1986. "Charlatans." [Contributed by Civil Rights Commission Chairman Clarence M. Pendleton, Jr.] [See MARTIN LUTHER KING]

Clar·i·fi·ca·tion (hē skrōōd up), n., 1966–88. The regular correction of misstatements, announced by aides after press

See **Church**

conferences or photo sessions in which the chief executive disobeys rules and responds to questions. [See BITBURG CEMETERY, BOLIVIA, BOMBING RUSSIA, DOMESTIC POLICIES, EUROPE, FOREIGN POLICIES, GERMANY, HOMELESS, HUNGER, IRANSCAM, LEAKS, MEMORY, MISSILE RECALL, MISSTATEMENT, NATIONAL HERO, NEVER, NUCLEAR FREEZE, ONE PLANE, RANSOM, SOCIAL SECURITY, STABLE DOLLAR, REYKJAVIK, SOUTH AFRICA, TAX INCREASE, WHEAT SALES, GREAT COMMUNICATOR]

Clas · si · fied ads (per′ son alz), n., The most reliable barometer of American unemployment. Despite a 10.8 percent jobless rate, the President noted that the *Washington Post*'s "Help Wanted" section filled an incredible twenty-four pages. [See SOGGY ECONOMY]

Clean out the sta · bles (lā′ offs), v., 1982. To flush away federal bureaucrats who "have been piling up." [See BUNCH OF CRAP]

Clean up the files (ub strukt′ jus′ tis), v., 1986. To tidy the White House basement by filing each report in its proper shredder. [Contributed by CIA Director William J. Casey]

Cleve · land, Grov · er (hōō?), n., 1. 1837–1908. The twenty-second President of the United States. 2. 1982. A great baseball pitcher the President recalls having "once played . . . in the movies." [Contributed by former Speaker of the House Tip O'Neill] [See GROVER CLEVELAND ALEXANDER, SENILITY]

Cold day in Ha · des (dōōmz′ dā), n., 1986. An unforeseeable time when the President shall become "soft on communism." [See NEVER, USEFUL IDIOT FOR KREMLIN PROPAGANDA]

Col · la · ter · al dam · age (nō′ bud ē wē nō), n., 1986. Civilians killed during air strikes or rescue missions. [See MINIMUM]

Col · lege stu · dents (kidz), n., 1966. A bunch of lazy, Godless good-for-nothings enrolled in "a four-year course in sex, drugs and treason." Someone should "harness their youthful energy with a strap." 2. 1987. A regiment of law-abiding, clean-cut champions in America's quest for excellence. "This generation is the best darn bunch of kids we ever had."

Col · or prob · lem (not hiz prob lem), n., 1965. "The bitter feelings engendered by extremists, both negro and white."

Com · mun · ism (lib′ ral izm), n., 1983. "The focus of evil in the modern world."

Com · mun · ists (kom′ ēēz), n., 1981. Fiends. "The only morality they recognize is what will further their cause, meaning they reserve unto themselves the right to commit any crime, to lie, to cheat." [See MARTIN LUTHER KING]

Com · mu · ni · ty chores (pun′ ish ment), n., 1968. Work that will make government freeloaders feel good about themselves.

Com · pet · i · tive · ness cam · paign (dī ver′ shun), n., 1987. A critical pride-in-America initiative that was scandalously overlooked by the handwringers in the leftist press, who prefer bad news about Iranscam. [See BITTER BILE IN MY THROAT]

Con · doms (shhh), n., 1987. Undefined, by order of U. S. Government, for fear of prompting mass orgies. [See DEEP DOO-DOO]

Con · gress (thugz), n., 1981–88. A "committee of 535" that loves to spend hard-earned taxpayers' dollars and write laws to torment businesses — and which refuses to debate America's Real Issue. [See REAL ISSUE]

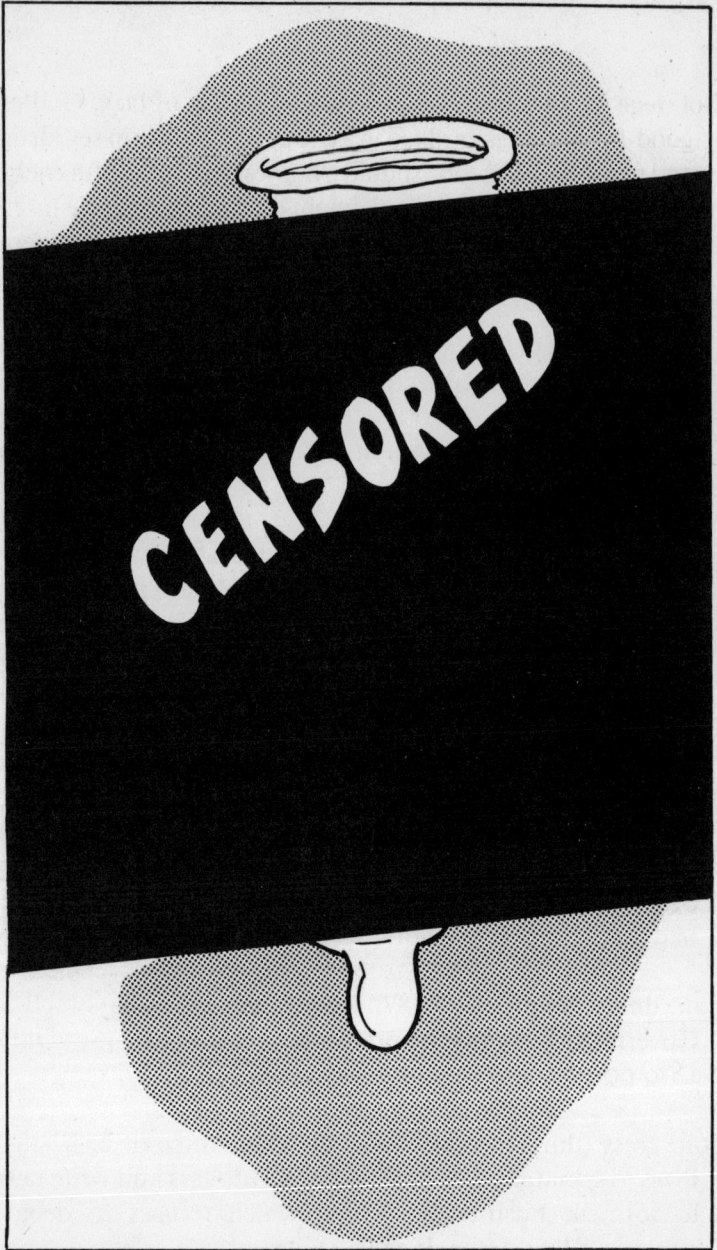

See **Condom**

Con·ser·va·tives (paks), n., 1964–88. Pro-life anticommunists who don't use drugs, distrust government hand-outs, treasure the American family, want God back in our schools and to whom "every day is the Fourth of July." [See LYNDON LA ROUCHE]

Con·spir·a·cy (duh lōō′ shunz) n., 1. 1949. A Soviet plot to take over the Screen Actors Guild. [See HELLCATS OF THE NAVY] 2. 1952. A Soviet plot to steal America's atomic bomb. [See ELECTRIC CHAIR, ROSENBERGS] 3. 1954. A Soviet plot to infiltrate Congress. [See JOE MCCARTHY] 4. 1966. A Soviet plot to corrupt American youth. [See HIPPY FREAKS] 5. 1968. A Soviet plot to undermine America's military effort in Vietnam. [See JANE FONDA] 6. 1975. A Soviet plot to act friendly in the guise of detente. [See DECADE OF NEGLECT] 7. 1976. A Soviet plot to steal America's Panama Canal. [See NOT ONE SQUARE INCH] 8. 1983. A Soviet plot to stop America's nuclear bomb tests. [See RED DAWN] 9. 1987. A Soviet plot to hurt people who spot Soviet plots, "making it unfashionable to be anticommunist." [See CONSPIRACY]

Con·stant down·beat (lā′ offs), n., 1982. The negative slant of news stories that would make you think America was in a recession or something. [See SOGGY ECONOMY]

Con·stant drum·beat (bod′ ē kounts), n., 1983. The chilling effect of news stories that would have you think we're fighting a secret war in Central America or something.

Con·struc·tive en·gage·ment (biz′ nus az yū′ shū al), n., 1984. The policy of sparking political change in South Africa by doing nothing. [See DETACHED MANAGEMENT STYLE]

Con·su·mer·ism (that *?!# nā′der), n., 1979. A form of Marxism that means "free enterprise is becoming far less free."

Con·tra aid vote (smōk skrēn), n., 1985. "The transcendent moral issue of our time." [See REAL ISSUE]

Con·tras (mer′sin aer ēz), n., 1982–88. A battalion of rock-jawed fighting machines — "the moral equivalent of our founding fathers and the brave men and women of the French Resistance" — who are using U. S. advice and humanitarian aid to drive the Soviets from Nicaragua once and for all. Their membership, which includes the President, receives millions of dollars from private donors. [See SLUSH FUND]

Cool·idge, Cal·vin (sound fuh mil′yer?), n., 1872–1933. The twenty-ninth President of the United States. His Republican administration is remembered for scandals by the secretary of the interior and attorney general, and tax cuts that fostered a brief economic boom prior to the Great Depression. [Contributed by the World Book Encyclopedia] [See WALL STREET CRASH]

Cour·age (man′hud), n., 1983. The spirit of fearlessness that would allow the government not to tax corporations. "When are we going to have the *courage* to point out that, in our tax structure, the corporate tax is hard to justify?" [See BUSINESS COMMUNITY]

Cov·ert ac·tion (shhh), n., 1981–88. A foreign policy that, however obvious to the country involved, must be kept secret from Americans.

Cow·boys (gud gīz), n., 1986. Unsung U. S. policy-makers within the National Security Council. [See RANSOM]

Crack (snort), n., 1986. A threat to humanity fended off by the President and the First Lady. [See NEWSWEEK, TIME]

Crap a pine · ap · ple (ouch), v., 1982. Meaning unknown. Asked by House Speaker Tip O'Neill to delay by three months a 10-percent tax cut, the President responded: "You're making me *crap a pineapple*." After someone suggested a 5-percent tax cut, the President substituted cactus. [See BELTWAY BLOODLETTING]

Cred · i · bil · i · ty (im′ ij), n., 1975. Believability. "Believe me, you must have *credibility*. . . Now you take my role in *Bedtime for Bonzo*. I was a scientist who raised a chimp as a child in my home. It was a huge moneymaker, terrific. People could believe in it. But then the studio decided to make a sequel called *Bonzo Goes to College*. I refused to play in it. It bombed. Who could believe a chimp could go to college and play on the football team? The whole thing lacked *credibility*." [See CRAP A PINEAPPLE]

Crim · in · al sus · pects (wī both′ ur with uh trī′ el?), n., 1985. Guilty people. "You don't have many *criminal suspects* who are innocent of a crime." [Contributed by Attorney General Edwin Meese III] [See MICHAEL DEAVER, RAY DONOVAN, CARL CHANNEL, EDWIN MEESE, LYN NOFZIGER, SLEAZE FACTOR]

Crip · ple (pluh sē′ bō), n., 1983. A necessary member of any governmental advisory commission. [Contributed by Secretary of the Interior James G. Watt] [See BLACK, TWO JEWS, WOMAN]

Crit · ics (rē port′ erz), n., 1982. "Paid political complainers."

Cru · el · ty (kon′ fi skāt yor li′ mō), n., 1985. "The natural expression of a communist government."

Cu · ba (bad gīz), n., 1966–88. An "outlaw state" [1985] run by "a roving wolf" [1984] who is "a liar" [1978] and "a client" of the Soviets [1987]. *Cuba* has a "basket-case economy" [1983] that is derived from "twin evils" [1986]: "exporting terrorism" [1982] and "peddling drugs like criminals, profiting on the misery of the addicted" [1983].

D

Dan·il·off, Nich·o·las (man from un′kl), n., 1986. An innocent hostage released by the Soviets, coincidentally, just as an evil Soviet spy was let go by America.

Dar·win's The·o·ry of E·vol·u·tion (sā′tin izm), n., 1980. A ludicrous idea soon to be proven false by "new evidence" heretofore concealed from the public. [See THE BIBLE]

Day Af·ter, The (wa′terd doun ver′shun), title, 1983. A far-fetched TV fantasy that tried to scare Americans into thinking nuclear war means the end of the world. [See REALISTS]

Deal (swap), n., 1985. An agreement America shall never make with evildoers. "The United States gives terrorists no rewards and no guarantees. We make no concessions. We make no *deals*." [See NEVER]

37

See **Deep Doo-doo**

Dea · ver, Mich · ael K. (ō kan′ a da), n., 1980–84. The former deputy White House chief of staff, who is credited with crafting the President's honest, fatherly image. [See ALCOHOLISM, PERJURY CONVICTION]

Dec · ade of neg · lect (ford and kar′ ter), n., 1986. The 1970s.

Deep doo-doo (num′ ber tōō), n., 1986. Technical term for adversity or trouble. Example: One does not want to be "in *deep doo-doo.*" [Contributed by Vice President George H. W. Bush] [See WIMP FACTOR]

Def · i · cit (hōō thuh hel kerz?), n., 1. 1966–81. An outrageous number ($60 billion) that reflects the uncontrolled spending binges of Democrats and liberals. [See TOTALITARIANISM] 2. 1982. A meaningless number ($180 billion) representing "the ironic by-product of our rapid and decisive success in bringing down the rate of inflation." 3. 1983–86. Definition unattempted. 4. 1987–88. An outrageous number ($150 billion) that reflects the uncontrolled spending binges of Democrats and liberals. [See GLOBAL DEPRESSION]

Dem · a · gog · uer · y (stiks and stōnz), n., 1982. Criticism of the President.

Dem · o · crat · i · za · tion (wôr), n., 1983. The process of neutralizing evildoers in Central America.

Dem · o · crats (bad gīz), n., 1980–88. "A pack of pessimists" [1984] who practice "pure demagoguery" [1981], are "so far left they've left America" [1984], brought about the national deficit [1966–88], "drove prayer out of our classrooms" [1982], and whose approach is "accompanied always by more government authority, less individual liberty, and ultimately, totalitarianism" [1984].

See **Detached management style**

40

De · ple · ted o · zone (thuh end iz nēēr), n., 1987. A thin layer of the atmosphere that offers an economic bonanza for America's skin-tanning lotion and hat-making industries. [Contributed by Secretary of the Interior Donald P. Hodel] [See PRESIDENT'S NOSE]

De · pres · sion (rē sesh′ un), n., 1980. The 7.4-percent unemployment rate under the Carter Administration. [See SOGGY ECONOMY].

De · sign · er gift en · sem · bles (ohh, for mē?), n., 1982. Elegant dresses that, until the leftist press raised a stink, were worn by the First Lady to boost the fashion industry and make Americans feel good about themselves again.

De · tails (pol′ is ēz), n., 1987. Trivia that "the President... is not a man for." [Contributed by Rear Admiral John M. Poindexter] [See IRANSCAM]

De · tached man · age · ment style (zzz), n., 1986. The art of running the federal goverment on two hours a day. [See WORK-ING VACATION]

De · tente (pēs), n., 1975. [French] The prelude to a Soviet sneak attack, from which America's "principal accomplishment seems to be our acquisition of the right to sell Pepsi-Cola in Siberia."

De · ter · rence (sē mī bom), n., 1966–88. The doctrine that enables America to end everything if anybody tries anything, ever, so there.

Dip · lo · ma · cy (aer strīk), n., 1981–88. Definition unknown.

Dip · sy dood · le (trōōth), n., 1982. A lie told by Democrats and liberals that deficits are "caused by our so-called massive tax cut and defense spending build-up. Well, that's a real *dipsy doodle*." [See MISSTATEMENT]

Di·rect ob·ser·va·tion (bath′ rōōm mon′ i terz), n., 1987. The condition under which federal workers must produce urine in pledging their allegiance to the war against illegal drugs.

Dis·ci·ples of weak·ness (buj′ it plan′ erz), n., 1986. Opponents of the Strategic Defense Initiative. [See DEFICIT]

Dis·ci·pline (klap′ ing ē rā′ serz), n., 1980–88. The most important subject that schools should learn American children.

Dis·cre·tion·ar·y fam·i·ly in·come (bred), n., 1982. Unnecessary spending money for poor people.

Dis·in·for·ma·tion (bil buk′ lē), n., 1. 1986. Important news released by the American government that "combines real and illusionary events." [Concocted by Rear Admiral John M. Poindexter] [See GREAT COMMUNICATOR] 2. 1987. Ruthless attacks by Democrats and liberals on the best darn Supreme Court nominee in this century. [See ROBERT BORK]

Di·ver·sion (il ē′ gl), n., 1. The secret flow of patriotic contributions from one slush fund to another. 2. [See PURPLE SILK DRESS, WALLACE BEERY]

Div·orce (al′ i mō nē), n., 1949. The inevitable result of marriage to actress Jane Wyman. [See EXTREME MENTAL CRUELTY]

Do·mes·tic spy·ing (big bruh′ ther), n., 1. 1975. A program needed to root out "an estimated 15,000 terrorists already organized into 21 groups in the United States." 2. 1981. An espionage program that absolutely will not be carried out on American citizens. [Contributed by White House

Counsellor Edwin Meese III] [See NEVER] 3. v., 1982–88. The rooting out of potential Soviet agents in America. [See BILL OF RIGHTS]

Dom·i·no (ev' rē wer), n., 1983. Any country on the planet that accepts American aid. [See EVIL EMPIRE]

Dooms·day plane (aer' fors wun), n., 1981. The President's specially equipped Boeing 747. Its nuclear bomb-launching capabilities offer a sense of security to all. [Contributed by White House aides] [See FOOTBALL]

Dou·ble build-down (nō chans), n., 1983. The President's first arms control proposal, which the Russians might have fallen for had Congress not picked it apart. [See CONSPIRACY]

Drag·on (mē n mī big mouth), n., 1987. A wrongful description of the First Lady's personality at various times. [Contributed by White House Chief of Staff Howard H. Baker, Jr.] [See HACKLES, GREAT LADY]

Drug-free A·mer·i·ca (por mē uh drink), n., 1986. The President's chief goal between August and nine P.M. November 4, 1986.

Drunk·en sail·ors (tip' sē ō nēl'), n., 1984. Democrats and liberals. [See TOTALITARIANISM]

Dum·my com·pan·ies (ak' mē), n., 1981. Phantom corporations set up by the CIA to combat potential communism at home and abroad. [See PEPSICO, AT&T, EXXON, BEATRICE]

Dump trucks (with bush on bord), n., 1983. The building blocks of an impenetrable security shield, erected around the White House after the liberation of Grenada. They since have been replaced by concrete fixtures, tastefully decorated with plants.

Dense pack (bōōm), n., 1983. The gathering of Peacekeeper missiles in one place to keep them safe from attack. [See ARMAGEDDON]

Dunce pack (BOOM), n., 1983. A phrase unworthy of definition. [See FLYING EDSEL, STAR WARS]

E

Ear · ly de · ploy · ment (b$\overline{ee}$ for' w$\overline{e}$ think tw$\overline{i}$s), n., 1987. The plan to install the Strategic Defense Initiative in outer space before it has been fully designed. [See FLYING EDSEL]

Eas · tern lib · er · al es · tab · lish · ment (n$\overline{oo}$ york t$\overline{i}$mz), n., 1980. An atheistic society of over-educated liberals and Democrats who own the leftist media and try to push elitist totalitarianism on hard-working folk. [See GEORGE BUSH]

E · co · nom · ic in · cen · tive meas · ures (with mir' erz), n., 1981. Plans to raise $22 billion without tax increases.

E · con · om · ic man · hood (hung l$\overline{i}$k uh hors), n., 1981. America's free-enterprise masculinity, which developing nations want to "strip us of." [Contributed by White House aides] [See WINDOW OF OPPORTUNITY]

E·lec·tion fraud (ō thōz prank′ sterz), n., 1986. Honest mistakes made in the Philippine *elections* by the Ferdinand Marcos camp. Of the gentlemen who pitched opposition votes into a ditch: "If he was really trying to get away with *fraud*, you'd think he'd have burned those ballots." [See MORALITY]

Em·er·ald neck·lace (werz rich′ erd al′ en?), n., 1986. A $60,000 string of jewels that Philippine First Lady Imelda Marcos said she gave to the Real First Lady. The Real First Lady denied receiving it. [See HONORARIUM]

E·mer·gen·cy aid (dōnt drop thuh krāt), n., 1983. Weapons.

E·mer·gen·cy change-of-ad·dress cards ("yōō mā bē uh win′ er!"), n., 1982. The U.S. Postal Service's plan to cope with nuclear war. [See SHOVEL]

En·dan·gered Spe·cies Act (man′ kind), n., 1978. A ridiculous law "which gives priority to tiny fish, weeds and spiders" over critical shopping malls and nuclear power plants. [See DEPLETED OZONE]

En·er·gy con·ser·va·tion (tern it up), n., 1980. A false answer to America's utility power problems that simply "means we'll all be too hot in the summer and too cold in the winter."

En·ti·tle·ments (skōōl lunch prō′ gramz), n., 1981. Addictive government handouts that rob American children of the hunger they'll need to succeed later in business. [See FOOD STAMPS]

En·vi·ron·ment·al ex·trem·ists (boi skouts), n., 1983. Critics of Secretary of the Interior James G. Watt.

See **Emergency change-of-address cards**

En·vi·ron·ment·al·ists (gurl skouts), n., 1982. "Left-wingers" who oppose "our very form of government" and seek "centralized planning and control of the society." [Contributed by Secretary of the Interior James G. Watt] [See NATION'S NUMBER-ONE ENVIRONMENTALIST]

E·qual Rights A·mend·ment (fū′ē), n., 1. 1972. A worthy idea that recognizes wives as *equals*. 2. 1976–88. A terrible idea that sees "sex and sexual differences treated as casually and amorally as dogs and other beasts treat them."

E·ra of vi·o·lent peace (dur′ tē li′ tl wôrz), n., 1986. The present. [Contributed by Chief of Naval Operations James Watkins]

Eth·ics in Gov·ern·ment Act (nun heer), n., 1978–88. A bureaucratic intrusion into the God-given right for a guy to earn a few extra bucks by working two jobs. [See WEDTECH]

Eu·rope (vā kā′ shun), n., 1981. An expendable buffer zone between freedom and totalitarianism, "where you could have the exchange of tactical weapons against troops in the field without its bringing either one of the major powers to pushing the button." [See LIMITED NUCLEAR WAR]

Ev·er·y·thing we can (huh?), n., 1984. What we are doing. [Contributed by the First Lady] [See MOMMY]

E·vic·tion (get out!), n., 1981. Notice that had to be served upon former President Jimmy Carter and his family, or else they'd likely be freeloading at the White House to this day. [Contributed by the First Lady] [See HOMELESS]

E·vil Em·pire (our grāt sā′ tin), n., 1983. The Union of Soviet Socialist Republics.

Ex · pan · sion of free · dom (kon′ kwest), n., 1986. The President's ultimate world goal: ''Not just the prevention of war but the *expansion of freedom.*''

Ex · treme men · tal cru · el · ty (bet shēz sor′ ē now), n., 1949. A ridiculous accusation by Jane Wyman that cost her the First Ladyship. [See ONE TOUGH SON OF A BITCH]

Eye · ball to eye · ball (bluhd′ shot), n., 1984. The only way to confront totalitarianism. [See NAP]

F

Fact · oids (wop′ erz), n., 1986. Snippets of fact-like information mentioned in Presidential speeches. [Contributed by White House aides]

Facts (fik′ shun), n., 1987. Information that often runs contrary to gut impressions, and thus is suspect. On the President's contention that America didn't swap arms for Iranian hostages: "My heart and best intentions still tell me that is true, but the *facts* and evidence tell me it is not." [See CLARIFICATION]

Fail · ure of so · cial · ism (nō prof′ its), n., 1983. What the economic state of American Indian reservations proves. [Contributed by Secretary of the Interior James G. Watt]

Fair · ness doc · trine (nō frē adz), n., 1936–87. An intrusion by government into the fundamental rights of broadcasters to air commercials for nuclear power.

Fair·ness is·sue (muh′ nē täkz), n., 1984. The trumped-up charge that the President's policies favor the rich. [See CATSUP]

Fall guy (tāk thuh rap), n., 1. 1986. Marine Lieutenant Colonel Oliver L. North [Contributed by CIA Director William J. Casey] 2. 1987. Rear Admiral John M. Poindexter. [Contributed by Mr. Casey] 3. 1987. Deceased former CIA Director William J. Casey. [Contributed by Mr. North and Mr. Poindexter]

Fas·cism (ful em ploi′ ment), n., 1976. The ideological basis for Franklin D. Roosevelt's New Deal programs in America.

Fer·rar·o, Ger·al·dine (gurl), n., 1. 1984. A "long overdue" female candidate for Vice President. 2. 1984. A $4 million something "that rhymes with rich" whose "little ass" was "kick[ed]." [Contributed by Mr. and Mrs. George H. W. Bush] 3. 1984. "The biggest bust politically in recent years." [Contributed by Presidential Campaign Manager Ed Rollins] [See CLARIFICATION]

Fic·tion (fakts), n., 1. 1967. Absurd claims by columnist Drew Pearson that a homosexual "ring" was operating in the governor of California's administration. "Complete *fiction*." [See KEMP] 2. 1986. Absurd claims by former Director of the Office of Management and Budget David A. Stockman that hardly anybody in White House knew what they were really doing. "I don't have much time for *fiction*." 3. 1987. Absurd claims by reporter Bob Woodward that hardly anybody in the White House knew what CIA Director William J. Casey was really doing. "Pure *fiction*." 4. 1987. Absurd claims in the press that the First Lady forced the dismissal of White House Chief of Staff Donald T. Regan. "Despicable *fiction*."

Filch (stēl), v., 1983. To playfully remove an unimportant briefing book from the Carter White House.

First strike (gä′ cha), n., 1981. The quick draw that is the key to winning nuclear war. [See ARMAGEDDON]

Flab · ber · gast · ed (uh wāk′), adj., 1986. Frustrated from trying to reason with democrats and liberals. [See TOTALITARIANISM]

Flat rate tax (in ā′ tē wun′, thuh rā′ gunz pād thrē per sent taks′ ez), n., 1979. How God makes His money, and how America should, too. "The Lord's share is considered to be one-tenth."

Food stamp di · et (al′ pō), n., 1983. Proof that hunger cannot exist in America. Fifty-six dollars' worth of handouts proved "quite adequate" for the Block family's week of culinary bliss. [Contributed by Secretary of Agriculture John R. Block]

Food Stamp Pro · gram (nō kum pren′ dā), n., 1982. A government plan to feed Puerto Ricans. [Contributed by Chairman of the President's Private Sector Survey on Cost Controls J. Peter Grace] [See CLARIFICATION]

Food stamps (hun′ grē kidz), n., 1987. Taxable income.

Foot · ball (thrō thuh bom), n., 1. 1981. Slang for a briefcase always within reach of the President that contains buttons to blow up the world, if need be. [See ARMAGEDDON] 2. 1981–88. A professional sport in which burly competitors vie for a congratulatory phone call from the President. [See HAVIZLAK]

For · eign a · gents (dem′ ō krats), n., 1982. Soviets who disguise themselves as priests and schoolteachers to infiltrate America's nuclear freeze campaign. [See READERS DIGEST]

For · eign pol · i · cy (kold wôr), n., 1981. To the Soviets: "Roses are red, violets are blue; stay out of El Salvador and Poland, too."

Found · ing fa · thers (sen yor' jef' er sun), n., 1985. A group of spunky eighteenth-century English colonists who foreshadowed the Contras. [See NUNS, SCHOOLBUSES]

Frank (yōō stink), adj., 1. 1981. Honest, pertaining to the nature of talks between American and Soviet leaders. [Contributationalized by Secretary of State Alexander M. Haig, Jr.] 2. n., 1966–88. The First Lady's favorite singer. [See MOB CONNECTIONS]

Free · dom fight · ers (kon' traz), n., 1986. Patriots everywhere who combat communism, no matter what it takes. [See NUNS, SCHOOLBUSES]

Free speech (pā az yōō spēk), n., 1966. A fundamental American right, as long as people watch what they say.

Friends (rich gīz), n., 1. 1981–88. Men who are eligible to be appointed to the Presidential cabinet. 2. 1983. Bombs. "Some of my best *friends* are MX missiles."

Full tech · no · log · i · cal pow · er (bomz uh wā'), n., 1967. The incendiary forces that America should unleash on Vietnam. [See ASH HEAP OF HISTORY]

Fun · da · men · tal · ly e · vil (red bash' ing), adj., 1986. Basically communist, pertaining to the "*fundamentally evil* way" Nicaragua is acting. [Contributed by Secretary of State George P. Shultz]

July 1988

R. Dig

How America Conquered Poverty
by President Ronald Reagan
PAGE 33

Quit Smoking through SEX
PAGE 100

Unforgettable Gene Rayburn
by Charles Nelson Reilly
PAGE 62

Contra Laffs, 17 — Life in T
Laughter, the Best Drug 59 — M
It Pays to Increase Your Weaponry
Cartoon captions — 83 Dull anecdot

67th Year: World's Most
Over 30,000,000,000,000 copies so

See **Free Speech**

55

Futz around

Futz a·round (al' mōst sed thuh ef' wurd), v., 1981. To antagonize. "How long has it been since anyone felt that way about our national government, that, by golly, you don't *futz around* with Uncle Sam." [See YOU DON'T STEP ON SUPERMAN'S CAPE]

G

Gal · a · tians (hē rōt it), n., 1986. A book of scripture quoted by the President in a Bible sent to butter up the Iranians. "'All the nations shall be blessed in you.' *Galatians* 3:38. Ronald Reagan, October 2, 1986."

Ga · zoo (kē′ stur), n., 1987. An unspecified orifice of the President's, into which the press would like to "stick" Iranscam. [Contributed by Senator Alan Simpson, R-Wyoming] [See CRAP A PINEAPPLE]

Gen · der Gap (kant liv with em), n., 1984. The periodic flow of feminine votes to Democrats and liberals. [See TOTALITARIANISM]

Ger · ma · ny (doich′ lund), n., 1985. A country that has nothing to do with Adolf Hitler. There are "very few alive that remember even the war, and certainly none of them who were adults and participating in any way." [See BITBURG CEMETERY]

57

See **God**

58

Ghor·ba·ni·far, Ma·nu·cher (rug mä′ kur), n., 1. 1986. A moderate Iranian merchant who tried to help America free the hostages. 2. 1986. A radical, lying cheat who leaked the story of America's attempt to free the hostages.

Gins·burg, Doug·las, H. (mēs′ ez chois′), n., 1987. An "enormously popular" U.S. judge who possesses a "tough, clear-eyed view" of law and order. [See E-Z WIDER, COMPUTER DATING, MEESE]

Gip·per (bon′ zō), n., 1. 1940–88. A movie character who periodically inhabits the President's body to plead for votes. Iranscam briefly exorcized it. "*The Gipper* has had some time in the penalty box, but now he's back on the ice." [Contributed by Senator Larry Pressler, R-South Dakota]

Glas·nost (dä, yōō awl), n., 1987. [Russian] An obviously fake "openness" policy in which Soviets try to explain away their nuclear power plant screw-ups by acting like Americans. [See LAUGHTER IN THE KREMLIN]

God (sur), n., 1984. An American with divine powers, without whom "democracy will not and cannot endure," who "has blessed our land and made us a good and caring people [and] should never have been expelled from America's classrooms." [See LIBERAL JUDGES]

God bless you (thats al fōks), n., 1981–88. The official sign-off to a Presidential address. [See CHURCH]

God·damn back, my (ga zōō′), n., 1986. The President's posterior, which he ordered the First Lady to "get off of," in response to her ceaseless lobbying to fire Chief of Staff Donald T. Regan. [Denied by the First Lady] [See HACKLES, LEECHES, GOD BLESS YOU]

God·fa·ther (yes sur), n., 1983. Edwin Meese III. [Contributed by former Environmental Protection Agency Assistant Administrator for Toxic Wastes Rita Lavelle]

Gor·bach·ev, Mik·hail (kä′mē), n., 1. 1986. A Communist dictator akin to Cuban President Fidel Castro, Libyan leader Moammar Gaddaffi and Palestine Liberation Organization leader Yassar Arafat. 2. 1987. An open-minded Soviet reformer who ought to tour America with the President.

Gosh (gyahsh), interjection, 1. 1982. As in "Shazam!" or "Jeepers!" An expression of astonishment. Contemplating the Middle East crisis over a map, the President measured with his fingers the distance between Israel and Lebanon and gasped: "*Gosh*, are they close!" 2. 1982. As in "God," a word to be invoked only in dire circumstances. Upon hearing that Nebraska Governor Charles Thone had lost reelection: "*Gosh* darn it." [See GODDAMNED BACK]

Gov·ern·ment (guv′munt), n., 1980. The problem.

Gramm-Rud·man (kuts), n., 1984–88. A masterful plan to curb the spending binges of Democrats and liberals, until it began to jeopardize America's outer-space peace umbrella.

Grand com·pro·mise (wē blōō it), n., 1986. An arms control agreement deftly avoided by the President at the Reykjavik Summit.

Great Com·mu·ni·ca·tor, The (uhhhh), n., 1983. Ronald Wilson Reagan. [See CLARIFICATION]

Great La·dy, a (bat′il aks), n., 1987. Nancy Davis Reagan. [Contributed by White House Chief of Staff Howard H. Baker, Jr.] [See HACKLES, DRAGON, CLARIFICATION]

See **Gorbachev**

Great prog · ress (to͞o steps bak), n., 1. 1982. Grand strides made in human rights during the regime of Ferdinand Marcos of the Philippines. [See OVERTHROW] 2. 1984. Grand strides made by the environment in the first three years of the President's administration. [See DEPLETED OZONE]

Great strides (wāt til nekst yeer), n., 1987. Grand progress made by blacks under the President's administration. [See CLARENCE M. PENDLETON, JR.]

Gre · na · da (ya ho͞o), n., 1. 1983. "A Soviet-Cuban colony being readied as a major military bastion to export terror and undermine democracy." 2. 1983–88. A great American military victory over "leftist thugs." [See ONE TOUGH SON OF A BITCH]

Grow · ing (ō nō!!), v., 1986. The tragic lengthening, due to gravity, of the First Lady's 1981 Inaugural gown, while on display. "Mrs. Reagan hasn't seen the dress, so she doesn't know how bad it might look, but she would like to be reassured that it is properly displayed for history's sake, the gown's sake, and the sake of the people who see it." [Contributed by the First Lady's Press secretary Elaine Crispen]

Guard · i · an (hand' lur), n., 1984. Former White House Spokesman Larry Speakes, whose commands the President had to obey. "My *guardian* says I can't talk."

Guer · ril · la war (pol' it iks), n., 1982. Teamwork within the White House. [Contributationalized by Secretary of State Alexander M. Haig, Jr.]

Guer · ril · la war · fare (heer wē gō a gen'), n., 1987. Teamwork within the White House. [Contributed by Secretary of State George P. Shultz]

See **Gosh**

Gun control

Gun con·trol (nō kun trōl′), n., 1983. The reduction of fire-
arms by jailing mobsters. "Hardcore criminals use guns,
and locking them up and throwing away the key is the best
gun control we could ever have."

H

Hack · les (klawz), n., 1987. An esoteric part of the First Lady's anatomy that, when in the "up" mode, transforms her into a "dragon." [Contributed by White House Chief of Staff Howard H. Baker, Jr.] [See BUM RAP, DRAGON, LEECHES]

Hang up (dī′ el tōn), n., 1986. The only way to deal with the First Lady on the phone. [Contributed by former Chief of Staff Donald T. Regan] [See HACKLES, DRAGON]

Har · lin · gen (wer?), n., 1985. A Texas village "just two days driving time" from terrorist Nicaragua.

Ha · vi · zlak (ha′ vuh luh chek), n., 1984. Boston Celtics basketball player John Havlicek, as pronounced by the President. [See NATION'S NUMBER-ONE SPORTS FAN]

Hel · lo (grrr!), n., 1986. The complete text of the President's remarks to Nicaraguan President Daniel Ortega at a United Nations gala reception. [See LITTLE DICTATOR]

Hell of a mess, a (oops), n., 1982. The funniest thing the President could say during a sound check for a speech about the American economy. . . "And I am prepared to tell you. It's *a hell of a mess.*" [See CONSTANT DOWNBEAT]

Hit list (en′ uh mēz), n., 1983. An inventory of Environmental Protection Agency workers who just don't appreciate the value of American corporations. [Contributed by EPA officials]

Hit squad (drēm), n., 1981. A quintet of Libyans sent by Colonel Moammar Gaddaffi to kill the President. The group is stiil at large. [See ONE TOUGH SON OF A BITCH]

Home Front (dad′ ē deer′ est), n., 1987. A fanciful novel written by the President's younger daughter concerning the far-fetched follies of a fictional First Family from California. [See FICTION]

Home · less, the (ī′ urn wēd), n., 1984. Nomads. They are "sleeping on grates. . . *homeless*, you might say, by choice."

Home · work (uh rith′ muh tik), n., 1984. Reading assigned by aides — "probably too much of it, without sitting back and relaxing" — that led to the President's confused performance in a debate with Democratic candidate Walter Mondale. [See MAKEUP]

Hon · o · ra · ri · um (brīb), n., 1981. The thousand-dollar fee paid to the National Security Advisor for an interview with the First Lady. [Contributed by National Security Advisor Richard V. Allen]

Hor · or show (jā′ son livz), n., 1982. A slide presentation that awakened the President to the Soviet buildup in El Salvador. [See PROJECT DEMOCRACY]

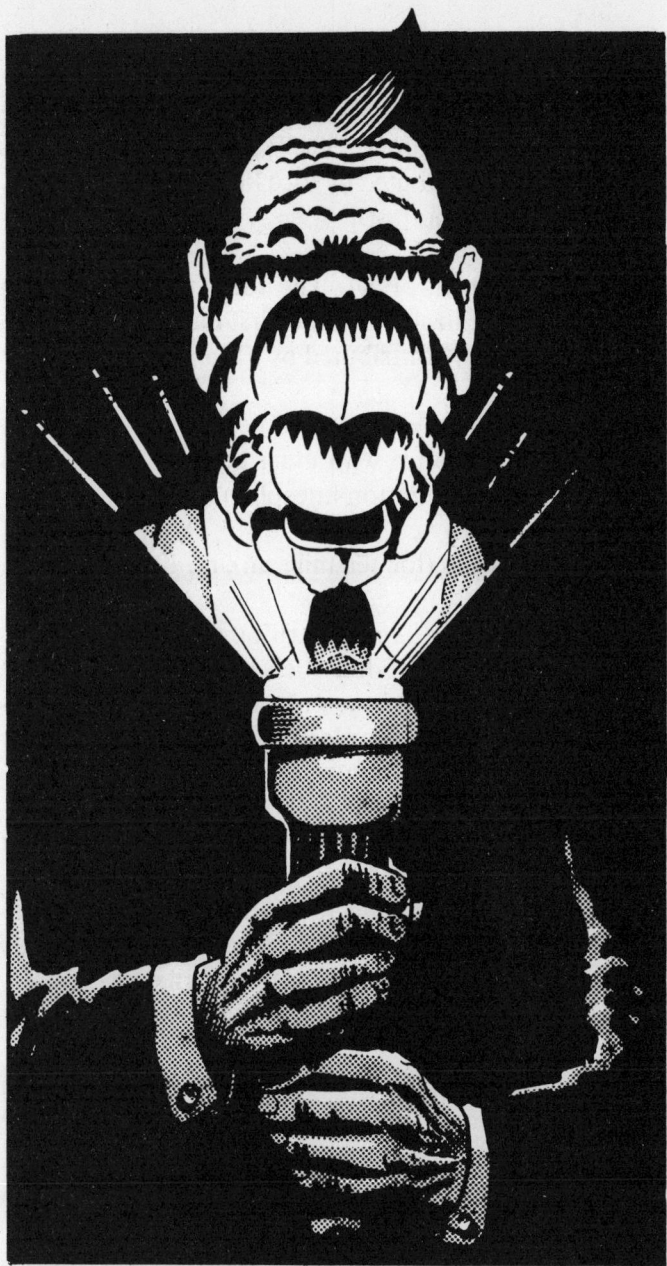

See **Hello**

Horse·rad·ish (hors′ shit), n., 1984. The awesome military might of the Soviet Union. "The Russians are as strong as *horseradish*." [Contributed by Vice President George H.W. Bush] [See DEEP DOO-DOO]

Hors·es (mis′ter ed), n., 1984. The topic of conversation whenever Queen Elizabeth II, the First Lady and the President get together. [Contributed by *Time* magazine]

Hos·tag·es (ē lek′ shun yēēr ish′ yōō), n., 1980. Fifty-two Americans held captive who must be remembered each day. 2. 1986–88. Definition unexplained.

Hu·man·i·tar·i·an aid (fôr′ tēn mil′ yun), n., 1984. Weapons.

Hun·ger (gosh), n., 1986. A malnutrition problem caused by ignorant poor people. "I don't believe that there is anyone going *hungry* in America by reason of denial or lack of ability to feed them; it is by people not knowing where or how to get this help." [See HOMELESS]

Hut·ton, E. F. ($$$$), n., 1984. A great brokerage firm that made an honest goof and happened to bilk banks and taxpayers out of $8 million. That its top officials pleaded guilty to wire and mail fraud charges is no cause to go printing their names in the papers. [Contributed by Attorney General Edwin Meese III]

Hys·te·ri·a (craaaaaaak!!), n., 1981–88. A public reaction that is never desired. [See NEVER]

I

Ice queen (hot tart), n., The former Director of the Environmental Protection Agency. 1. 1983. Anne McGill Gorsuch. Under criticism, she said: "I don't melt at the first macho scream, and I'm not melting now." She later resigned from the EPA. 2. 1984. Anne Gorsuch Burford. Appointed a candidate for the National Advisory Committee on Oceans and Atmosphere, she called the job a "nothing burger" and withdrew her name. [See PURPLE SILK DRESSES]

Il·le·gal (im or′ il), adj., 1966–88. [See IMMORAL]

Im·mor·al (il ē′ gil), adj., 1966–88. [See ILLEGAL]

In charge (for′ tē winks), adj., 1981. To be reclining horizontally with eyes closed, at full attention. After U.S. planes downed two Libyan fighter jets, "the President was *in charge*, and if there had been any action he needed to take, he would have been awakened." [Contributed by White House Counsellor Edwin Meese III] [See DETACHED MANAGEMENT STYLE]

See **In charge**

In·come tax (ben dō vur), n., 1966. A federal moneymaking scam that "was created by Karl Marx. It has no justification in getting government revenue."

In con·trol (dik′ tā ter), adj., 1981. To have taken over the government in order to reassure a frightened nation. "I am *in control*." [Contributationalized by Secretary of State Alexander M. Haig, Jr.]

In·de·pend·ent coun·sel (not tōo in dē pen′ dent), n., 1. 1986. A special prosecutor who should be appointed to ensure fairness for former White House Deputy Chief of Staff Michael K. Deaver. [Contributed by Mr. Deaver] 2. 1987. A special prosecutor who should be dismissed to ensure fairness for former White House Deputy Chief of Staff Michael K. Deaver. [Contributed by Mr. Deaver] [See PERJURY]

In·fla·tion (siks′ tē sent toot′ zē rōl), n., 1. 1965–80. The economic consequences of deficit spending. [See DEFICIT] 2. 1981–88. The economic consequence of deficit spending in previous administrations. [See DEFICIT]

In·for·ma·tion (pow′ er), n., 1. 1984. Data that the President has "a better store of. . .than a President usually has." 2. 1986. Data that the President has less of than a president usually needs. [Contributed by the Tower Commission] 3. 1984. Data that the CIA no longer has to supply to American citizens.

I·N·F treaty (red her′ ing), n., 1987. An arms control victory over those gullible Russians. They think it says America can't build her outer-space peace umbrella. But we will anyway!

In · ter · est-free loans (shā′ dē dēl), n., 1984. A worthless $60,000 advance to White House Counsellor Edwin Meese III from a friend who just happened to be named later to the U.S. Postal Service Board. "The idea there was any connection between the loan and the recommendation . . . was so far from my thoughts it never occurred to me . . . It never occurred to me that an *interest-free loan* was a thing of value." [Contributed by Mr. Meese]

In · ter · est rates (not in′ ter est ed), n., 1984. Numbers that have "no connection" to the federal budget deficit. [See STOCK MARKET COLLAPSE]

In · tol · er · ance (hyōō′ man ism), n., 1984. The hatred of churches that led liberals and Democrats to ban prayers from American schools. "Isn't the real truth that they are *intolerant* of religion? They refuse to tolerate its importance in our lives." [See CHURCH, TOTALITARIANISM]

I · ran (per′ sha), n., 1. 1980. A nation of terrorists that America should never deal with. 2. 1986. A nation of rug-makers who seem like reasonable men. 3. 1987. A nation of terrorists that America should never deal with. [See NEVER]

I · ran · scam (wa′ ter gāt), n., 1986. A "bolt from the blue" that distracted Congress and the press from the essential business of government.

See **In control**

J

Jew·el·ry (dī′mundz), n., 1986. Shiny little things that American women are not "prepared to give up" in exchange for economic sanctions against South Africa. [Contributed by White House Chief of Staff Donald T. Regan]

John Birch So·ci·e·ty (hē ak sep′ted thuh en dors′ment), n., 1965. A cadre of pure Americans who aren't afraid to speak out about the Soviet infiltration of California government. [See FLUORIDE]

Joint ex·er·cis·es (wôrz), n., 1984. American military campaigns that include at least one soldier from another country. Although commonly viewed as a U.S. rescue mission, the Grenadan campaign couldn't have been won without crack troops from the following allies: Antigua, Barbados, Dominica, Jamaica, St. Lucia and St. Vincent. [See PEACEKEEPERS, RESCUE MISSION]

Ju·di·cial re·straint (hang em), n., 1. 1985. What federal judges should practice: forget this nonsense about constitutional law and just put the bad guys in jail. [See CRIMINAL SUSPECTS]

Jun·gle (wätz), n., 1966. The shadowy, terrifying American city. "Every day, the *jungle* draws a little closer... Our city streets are *jungle* paths after dark." [See POTENTIAL ENTERPRISE ZONES]

Jus·tice (pā as yōo go), n., 1980–88. An ideal that can only be achieved by giving the President what he wants. Example: Supreme Court nominee Douglas H. Ginsburg would have been confirmed immediately "if there were any kind of *justice* in Washington." [See GINSBURG]

K

Keis·ter (ga zo͞o′), n., 1981. An unspecified orifice that the President has "had it up to" with "leaks." [See CRAP A PINEAPPLE]

Ken·ne·dy, John F. (gōst), n., 1. 1960. A contemptible snake who, beneath a "tousled boyish haircut," offers ideas that are "still old Karl Marx" and remindful of Hitler. 2. 1984. A great President who, if alive today, "would be ashamed of those in the liberal Democratic leadership who would weaken our defense, endanger our security and sell out the cause of freedom in Latin America." [See GRAVE-ROBBING]

Ken·ne·dy, Ted (fat′ sō), n., 1983. The anti-Christ, whose totalitarian tentacles extend everywhere. When Missouri officials pressed for compensation for dioxin victims, they were "playing right into the hands of *Ted Kennedy.*" [Contributed by Environmental Protection Agency Assistant Administrator for Toxic Wastes Rita Lavelle]

See **Kennedy, Ted**

Kick a lit · tle ass (yuh big bul′ ē), v., 1984. Win a debate with a girl. [Contributed by Vice President George H. W. Bush] [See MANHOOD]

King, Mar · tin Lu · ther (nō bel′ pēs priz), n., 1929–68. 1. 1983. A negro leader whose popularity is "based on image, not reality" and who may have been a Communist, according to FBI files that will remain sealed until the turn of the century. "We'll know in about thirty-five years, won't we?" [See COMMUNISTS] 2. 1986. "A drum major for justice." 3. 1987. "Martin Lucifer Coon," according to White House aides. [Contributed by former Secretary of Education Terrel H. Bell]

Kis · sin · ger Com · mis · sion (tō′ dēz), n., 1983. A distinguished panel of respected public servants who says it's okay to hold a war in El Salvador.

Kitch · en cab · i · net (ben uh fak′ terz), n., 1981. A few trusted friends, such as retailer Alfred Bloomingdale and brewer Joseph Coors, who advise the President on key issues, like retailing and brewing. [See MILLIONAIRES]

See **Leading the way**

L

Lame duck (kwak), n., 1986. A weak leader, which the President shall never be. [See BORK, GINSBURG, WALL STREET CRASH]

Land·slide (tē´vē prō jek´shunz), n., 1984. A 54 percent margin in an election where 53 percent of America's registered voters cast ballots.

Lar·yn·gi·tis (dōnt ask), n., 1987. A temporary illness that prohibits the President from answering questions about arms transfers. [See CLARIFICATION]

Laugh·ter in the Krem·lin (nyuk nyuk), n., 1983. What happens when anything bad occurs.

Lead·ing the way (ting´kl), v., 1986. Urinating into a cup to personally launch a four-month-long crusade against drugs. [See DIRECT OBSERVATION]

Leaks (shhh), n., 1. 1980–88. The flow of information between the government and reporters. 2. 1987. Slang for a key component of the President's mandatory drug testing program. 3. 1982. The President's greatest disappointment: "The inability to control the *leaks*." [See LEADING THE WAY]

Leech · es (hang up on mē, wil hē?), n., 1987. Troublemakers. "I don't think most people associate me with *leeches* or how to get them off. I'm an expert at it." [Contributed by First Lady Nancy Reagan, to a group of Girl Scouts, following the resignation of Chief of Staff Donald T. Regan]

Left · ist thugs (pe′ zents), n., 1983. Grenadans who threatened six-hundred Americans and forced a 6,000-troop rescue mission. [See RESCUE MISSION]

Lib · er · al jud · ges (līk bork), n., 1986. [See SOCIOLOGY MAJORS]

Lib · er · als (redz), n., 1983. The opposite of Americans. [Contributed by Secretary of the Interior James G. Watt]

Lib · er · als of the Jew · ish com · mu · ni · ty (kom′ ē jōōz), n., 1982. Citizens of Israel who "will weaken our [U.S.] ability to be a good friend of Israel." [Contributed by Secretary of the Interior James G. Watt]

Light · ed can · dles (pē ar), n., 1981. The President's hard-line stance to drive the Soviets out of Poland.

Lim · it · ed im · mu · ni · ty (tāk thuh fith), n., 1987. The legal protection granted to Lieutenant Colonel Oliver L. North and Rear Admiral John M. Poindexter so that they could set Congress straight on American priorities.

Lim·it·ed nu·cle·ar war (win wun for thuh gip′er), n., 1982. A minor exchange of atom bombs between superpowers. It "may not be desirable." [Contributed by White House Counsellor Edwin Meese III] [See ARMAGEDDON]

Line-i·tem ve·to (dik′tā ter ship), n., 1980–88. The power to control runaway spending that Congress consistently denies the President. With it, welfare lard could be cut from government without penalizing America's starving military. [See HUNGER, STAR WARS]

Lit·tle dic·ta·tor (shor′tē), n., 1985. President Daniel Ortega of Nicaragua.

Lit·tle House on the Prai·rie (mas′ter pēs thē′uh ter), n., 1981. Television's finest hour. This spellbinding series depicts a true-to-life family strengthened by American values in the days before Democrats and liberals. [See HIGHWAY TO HEAVEN]

Lit·tle lynch mob (mod′er ets), n., 1986. The half of Congress that opposed U.S. District Court Justice nominee Daniel Manion. [See LYNCH MOB]

Long o·ver·due cor·rec·tion (krash!), n., 1987. A one-day drop in the Dow Jones Industrial Index by 508 points. [See HERBERT HOOVER]

Loon·ey tunes (thats al fōks), n., 1986. The ridiculous notion that jobs for girls should pay as much as jobs for men. [Contributed by Civil Rights Commission Chairman Clarence M. Pendelton, Jr.] [See GENDER GAP]

Low-lev·el munch·kin (bad gurl), n., 1983. Former Justice Department Special Assistant Barbara Honegger, who quit her job and called the President's sex discrimination policies "a sham." [Contributed by Justice Department spokesman Tom DeCair]

Ly·ing (spēk′ing), n., 1987. 1. A diplomatic tool that saves
lives. [Contributed by Lieutenant Colonel Oliver L. North]
[See HOME SECURITY SYSTEM, SPOT ADS, OBSTRUCTION OF
JUSTICE, ULTIMATE COVERT ACTIVITY, SHREDDER PAR-
TY] 2. [See DEAVER, PERJURY]

Lynch mob (thuh kun′ trē), n., 1. 1974. The Congressional ma-
jority that favored the resignation of President Richard M.
Nixon. 2. 1987. The Senate majority that opposed Supreme
Court Justice nominee Robert H. Bork. [See MODERATE]

M

Mad dog (ra′ bid), n., 1. 1967. A resident of Detroit who takes part in a race riot. "Lawbreakers and *mad dogs.*" [See Potential Enterprise Zone] 2. 1986. Colonel Moammar Gaddaffi of Libya. 3. 1986. Ronald Wilson Reagan of America. [Contributed by Mr. Gaddaffi] [See So'ze Yer Mom]

Mag · ic as · ter · isk (big lī), n., 1986. The punctuation mark that balanced the 1982 federal budget. Placed beside a $44 billion deficit, it referred readers to a note that said "future savings to be identified." [Confessed by former Director of the Office of Management and Budget David A. Stockman] [See Triumph of Politics]

Mag · ic of the mar · ket · place (lā′ zā fer), n., 1982. The natural tendency of economic problems to go away if left alone. [See Detached Management Style]

Mag·ic word, the (muh′ nē), n., 1979. "Decontrol."

Make my day (dī muh′ ther), exclamation, 1985. 1. A warning to street punks everywhere. [Contributed by Carmel, California, Mayor Clint Eastwood] [See SUDDEN IMPACT] 2. A warning to Congressional punks everywhere. "I have only one thing to say to the tax increasers. Go ahead, *make my day*." [See MR. SMITH GOES TO WASHINGTON]

Make·up (grē′ shun form′ yōō luh), n., 1984. Girlie stuff the President refuses to wear. Asked why he looked tired in a debate with Democratic candidate Walter Mondale: "If I had as much *makeup* on as he did, I'd have looked younger too." [See UM HUMM]

Make work pro·grams (jobz), n., 1981. The needless construction of highways and sewers.

Ma·jor in·sur·gen·cy (krī wulf), n., 1981. The potential Soviet-sponsored bloodbath that America has uncovered in Guatemala, yet those ingrates still don't want our peacekeeping missionaries. [See RESCUE MISSION]

Male bas·tion (menz klub), n., 1984. White House politics. [Contributed by former United Nations Ambassador Jeanne K. Kirkpatrick]

Man·date for change (wun out uv āt), n., 1981. A 50.7 percent margin in the Presidential election of 1980. Twenty-seven percent of America's adult population voted.

Man·hood (jon wayn), n., 1. 1981. An unquestioned attribute of Ronald Reagan, Jr., despite his decision to become a ballet dancer. "It's OK. We made sure he's all *man*." 2. 1984. A measurable source of personal pride to Vice President George H. W. Bush: "I'll lay my record on any forum, whatever it is, on the *manhood*, up against his [Democratic Presidential candidate Walter Mondale's]." [Contributed by Mr. Bush] [See TINY LITTLE GUN]

Mar · gin of su · per · i · or · i · ty (gap), n., 1983. The difference in size between the Soviet and American missile arsenals. [See MANHOOD]

Mar · riage (yes deer), n., 1940–49. A lifetime vow of togetherness. [See JANE WYMAN] 2. 1952– . A lifetime vow of togetherness. [See NANCY DAVIS REAGAN] 3. 1987. A good reason for Americans to be tested for the AIDS virus. [See CONDOM]

Marx · ism (pyo͞or ē′ vl), n., 1964. "The most dangerous enemy ever known to man." [See TED KENNEDY]

Mashed po · ta · to cir · cuit (kok′ tāl brunch′ ez), n., 1982. The mushy road traveled by God's emissary to the White House.

Meese, Ed · win, III (big ed), n., 1965–87. A cherished White House counsellor and great attorney general. [See AIDS, APPEARANCE PROBLEM, CENSORSHIP, DEBATEGATE, DRUGS, EXTORTION, GODFATHER, HIGH ROLLERS, IL-LEGAL, IMMORAL, INCOMPETENCE, INTEREST-FREE LOAN, IRANSCAM, MERRILL LYNCH, MIRANDA, OBESITY, PAPER SHREDDER, PORNOGRAPHY, SLEAZE FACTOR, SUR-VEILLANCE, TEAMSTERS, WIRE TAPS, WEDTECH]

Mem · o · ry (uh . . .), n., 1. 1982. A mental faculty lost by National Security Advisor Richard V. Allen when asked if he reported a gift from Japanese journalists he received for arranging an interview with the First Lady. [Contributed by Mr. Allen] 2. 1984. A mental faculty lost by Counsellor Edwin Meese III when asked if he had ever seen one of Jimmy Carter's briefing books during the 1980 Presidential campaign. [Contributed by Mr. Meese] 3. 1984. A mental faculty lost by CIA Director William J. Casey when asked if he had ever seen one of Jimmy Carter's briefing books during the 1980 Presidential campaign. [Contributed by Mr. Casey] 4. 1986. A mental faculty lost by Supreme Court Justice William Rhenquist when asked if he systematically challenged black voter registrations during the 1960s. [Contributed by Justice Rhenquist] 5. 1987. A mental faculty lost by the President when asked if he approved arms shipments to Iran. 6. 1987. A mental faculty lost by Lieutenant Colonel Oliver L. North. "My *memory* has been shredded." [Contributed by Mr. North] 7. 1988. A mental faculty lost by Vice President George Bush when asked to whom he bitched about the sale of arms to Iran. [See DEEP DOO-DOO]

Mem · os (dōō not ō′ pen), n., 1986. Documents that jeopardize the President. [See SMOKING GUN]

Men (MEN!), n., 1. 1965–88. People who never have abortions. 2. 1983. Creatures who would still be "walking around in skin suits, carrying clubs" were it not for girls.

Men · tal · ly a · lert (not brān ded), adj., 1984. A doctor's reassuring description of the President after a televised debate with Democratic candidate Walter Mondale. [See SENILITY]

Mice (rats), n., 1987. Aides to White House Chief of Staff Donald T. Regan. [Contributed by White House aides] [See LEECHES]

Mil · i · tar · y ad · vi · sors (sē ī ā), n., 1983. American troops fighting in secret foreign wars.

Mil · lion · aires (kun trib′ yōō terz), n., 1980–88. Men who tell the President what to do.

See **Meese**

Mines (em bar′ gō), n., 1. 1984. A peacetime weapon that should choke off Nicaragua's Soviet connection and keep those leftist thugs off balance. [See BOLAND AMENDMENT] 2. 1987. The coward's way to do battle in the Persian Gulf. Why can't those darn Iranians stand up and fight like men? [See MEN]

Min·i·mum (a fyōō heer and ther), n., 1981–88. What collateral damage is always "held to." In a strike against Libya: "Only one to two percent of the bombs impacted in civilian areas." [See COLLATERAL DAMAGE]

Min·i·mum wage (werk′ing pôr), n., A U.S. law that "has caused more misery and unemployment than anything since the Great Depression." [See CALVIN COOLIDGE] The minimum wage under the President is as follows:

> 1981: $3.35 per hour
> 1982: $3.35 per hour
> 1983: $3.35 per hour
> 1984: $3.35 per hour
> 1985: $3.35 per hour
> 1986: $3.35 per hour
> 1987: $3.35 per hour
> 1988: $3.35 per hour

Min·i·me·mos (līt rēd′ing), n., 1982. Single-page reports to the President that summarize major issues. [See PLAUSIBLE DENIABILITY]

Mis·sery mer·chants (bil moi′ erz), n., 1982. Leftist reporters who just aren't happy unless they're interviewing some jobless basket case who's down on America.

See **Missile recall**

Mis · sile re · call (sī' ens fik' shun), n., 1982. America's unquestioned ability to turn around nuclear warheads in mid-flight. "They can be *recalled* if there has been a miscalculation." [See CLARIFICATION]

Mis · state · ment (ad lib), n., 1981–88. The declaration that precedes a "clarification." Example: When the President told a news conference Israel was not involved in arms shipments to Iran, it was "just a *misstatement* that I didn't realize that I had made...when I finished bumping my head, I said, 'Quick. Write down a correction of this!' " The clarification: "There may be some misunderstanding of one of my answers tonight." [1986]

Mis · take (nō big dēl), n., 1987. The sale of weapons to Iranian terrorists accompanied by the skimming off of profits to make payments to the Contras.

Mix (but dōnt mer' ē), n., 1983. The most critical aspect to government advisory commissions. We have "every *mix* you can have. I have a black. I have a woman, two Jews and a cripple." [Contributed by Secretary of the Interior James G. Watt]

Mod · er · ates (neks tōō a til' uh), n., 1986. People whose views fall in the middle of the political spectrum. Examples:
1. 1964. Barry Goldwater
2. 1968. Richard Daley
3. 1972. Richard M. Nixon
4. 1973. Spiro T. Agnew
5. 1975. Henry Kissinger
6. 1977. Nicaraguan General Anastasio Somoza
7. 1978. General Augusto Pinochet of Chile
8. 1980. Ronald Wilson Reagan
9. 1981. James G. Watt

10. 1982. Ferdinand Marcos
11. 1983. Jose Napolean Duarte
12. 1984. Ronald Wilson Reagan
13. 1985. Edwin Meese
14. 1986. The Iranian government
15. 1987. Robert H. Bork
[See PATRICK BUCHANAN, WILLIAM F. BUCKLEY, JR., PAUL HARVEY, JOSEPH MCCARTHY, GEORGE WILL]

Mod·ern·iz·a·tion (spend thuh buks), n., 1985. The manufacture of new and better bombs.

Mom·my (deer′est), n., 1952–88. The First Lady.

Mon cher Ron (wut uh gī), n., 1982. [French] The President. [Contributed by French President Francois Mitterrand]

Mon·dale, Wal·ter (grrrr), n., 1976–84. A Democrat and a liberal. [See TOTALITARIANISM]

Mor·al ma·jor·i·ty (jeh′rē fal′wel), n., 1980–88. A group of outstanding patriots who practice anticommunism each Sunday.

Mor·e·no, or Mon·or·em (ho͞o cerz), n., 1986. One of South Africa's "most prominent Black leaders" and a solid supporter of the President.

Moth·er to moth·er cam·paign (giv us uh barf bag), n., 1986. The First Lady's tour of Asia to combat drugs. [See GREAT WALL, SHOPPING]

Mur·der board (jorj wil), n., 1982. White House aides who play the parts of unsavory reporters in the final dress rehearsal before a show. [Contributed by White House aides] [See PRESS CONFERENCE]

M·X Mis·sile (big wun), n., 1983. The Peacekeeper nuclear bomb, "the right *missile* for the right time." Rejection by Congress would have been "a blow to our national security that no foreign power would ever have been able to accomplish." [See AIM AT MOSCOW AND LAND ON CHICAGO]

N

Nan·cy·ism (wipd), n., 1987. A desire to negotiate with Soviets that is implanted in the President's head via the First Lady's horrifying power of mind control. [Contributed by the White House staff]

Nap (wirk), n., 1980–88. An energy-efficient state of awareness that follows lunch. This ensures that the President will be razor sharp in case of sneak attack. "If our planes were shot down, yes, they'd wake me up right away. If the other fellows were shot down, why wake me up?" [1981] [See IN CHARGE]

Na·tion·al mo·bil·i·za·tion (mē′ dē uh blits), n., 1986–87. A crusade against the brain-dissolving drug crack that began in July, lasted well into Election Day and was punctuated the following January with the slashing of $913 million in fat from the federal drug enforcement budget.

Na·tion·al Wil·der·ness Ar·e·as (wudz), n., 1979. Public land whose beauty is exploited by the elite few who are "robust enough to go backpacking." [See FOR SALE]

Na·tion's num·ber-one en·vi·ron·men·tal·ist (for shām), n., 1982. Secretary of the Interior James G. Watt [Contributed by Mr. Watt] [See DEPLETED OZONE, DRILLING RIGHTS, OFFSHORE OIL LEASING, POLLUTION, SALE OF NATIONAL FORESTS, STRIP MINING, ENVIRONMENTALIST]

Na·tion's num·ber-one sports fan (strīk fôr), n., 1984. The President. [Contributed by CBS Commentator Brent Musberger] [See FOOTBALL, HAVIZLAK]

Neat i·de·a (til yo͞o get cawt), n., 1987. The keen notion of selling okay stuff to Iranians so we can buy swell stuff for our Contra guys. [Conceptualized by Lieutenant Colonel Oliver L. North]

Neu·tron weap·on (deth), n., 1978. A clean bomb that won't kill innocent buildings and cars.

Nev·er (af' ter thuh ē lek' shun), n., 1984–88. Probably. 1. 1984. On tax increases: "A president should *never* say *never*, but I'm going to violate that rule and say *never*." [See USERS FEES, REVENUE ENHANCEMENT MEASURES, TAX REFORM] 2. 1985. On hostages: "Americans will *never* make concessions to terrorists. To do so would only invite more terrorism." [See ARMS TRANSFER, IRANSCAM]

New fed·er·al·ism (yo͞o tāk it), n., 1982. A long overdue American policy that allows each state to decide just how hungry its children should be.

New glo·bal·ism (wôrz bi prok' sē), n., 1986. The foreign policy of making sure that freedom fighters everywhere can always count on a paycheck. [See FREEDOM FIGHTERS]

See **Nancyism**

News re · ports (yū es ā tōō dā′), n., 1981–88. 1. Lies. Example: "I've never heard such dissemination of misinformation (regarding Iranscam) since I've been here." [See WASHINGTON POST] 2. 1986. Information. Example: "I watch every day like everybody else to find out what will come out (regarding Iranscam)." [See WASHINGTON TIMES]

News sour · ces (bil kā′ sē), n., 1. 1982. Nameless villains who are "betraying this country" by speaking to reporters. [Contributed by White House Counsellor Edwin Meese III] 2. 1987. Nameless villains who "very seriously compromised" America's seizure of the Achille Lauro hijackers. [Contributed by Lieutenant Colonel Oliver L. North] 3. Lieutenant Colonel Oliver L. North. [Contributed by *Newsweek* magazine] [See ACHILLE LAURO]

New · ton, Wayne (don′ ka′ shān), n., 1984. A fabulous entertainer who is loved by all. [Contributed by Secretary of the Interior James G. Watt] [See WRONG ELEMENTS]

New un · em · ploy · ment rate (in′ stant drop), n., 1983. An improved statistic that counts 1.67 million military personnel as part of America's workforce. With this *new* calculation, the *unemployment rate* dropped from 10.7 percent in December of 1982 to 10.2 percent the following month. [See SOGGY ECONOMY]

Nic · ar · ag · ua (vē et nam′), n., 1983–88. A Soviet satellite that threatens to export communism to nearby Harlingen, Texas.

Nic · a · ra · guan Dem · o · crat · ic Re · sist · ance (our gīz), n., 1987. "The so-called Contras. . . people, living, breathing, young men and women, who have had to suffer." [Contributed by Lieutenant Colonel Oliver L. North] [See A HUNDRED MILLION DOLLARS]

Just see **No**

Nice so·lid prof·it (fif′ tē per sent′), n., 1983. America's wish for her trusted defense contractors. [Contributed by Secretary of the Navy John Lehman] [See DEFICIT]

Ni·dal, A·bu (for thuh werld champ′ ē un ship), n., 1987. A beast from the Middle East whom Lieutenant Colonel Oliver L. North will wrestle any time, any place. [Contributed by Mr. North] [See SERGEANT SLAUGHTER]

Nine-to-five fight·ing (bool′ sheet, muh fuh′), n., 1983. The Salvadoran army's disgracefully unprofessional approach to war. [Contributed by White House aides.]

No (ix′ nā), interjection, 1. 1980. "The best form of birth control." 2. 1986. The solution to drug abuse. "Just say *No.*" [Contributed by the First Lady]

No·bel Peace Prize (os′ ker), n., 1987. An award the President deserves, based on his tireless work in Central America and the Middle East. [Contributed by the First Lady] [See ARIAS PEACE PLAN]

Noise based on ig·no·rance (bich bich bich), n., 1983. Criticism of the President. [See DEMAGOGUERY]

Non·le·thal aid (gunz that dōnt werk), n., 1986. [See HUMANITARIAN AID]

North, Ol·i·ver L. (blud n guts), n., 1. 1986. "A national hero." [See ASS] 2. 1987. A "loose cannon." [Contributed by White House aides] [See RANSOM] 3. 1987. An "old buffoon." [Contributed by best friend Betsy North] [See PARKLANE HOSIERY] 4. 1987. "Every secretary's dream of a boss." [Contributed by personal secretary Fawn Hall] [See SHREDDING PARTY]

Note · keep · ing (dūd′ ling), n., 1987. A revolutionary new concept in compiling records that was installed in the White House as a result of Iranscam. [See MEMORY]

Not one square inch (blok that kik), n., 1984. The amount of turf that Freedom lost to Communism during the President's first four years. [See FOOTBALL]

Nu · cle · ar al · ler · gy (hē rō′ shē ma), n., 1985. The inexplicable aversion that countries like Japan hold toward atomic bombs. [See MEMORY]

Nu · cle · ar freeze (kā jē bē), n., 1982. A disarmament movement inspired "by some who want the weakening of America and who are manipulating many honest people and sincere people." [See CONSPIRACY]

Nu · cle · ar tests (kan′ ser), n., 1985. The only way we know those darn bombs really go off, and that the taxpayers are getting their money's worth.

Nu · cle · ar warn · ing shot (in san′ i tē), n., 1981. A bomb to be dropped for "demonstrative purposes." [Contributationalized by former Secretary of State Alexander M. Haig, Jr.] [See NEVER]

Nu · cle · ar waste (put it in thuh ō′ shun), n., 1979. A fascinating by-product of the atomic energy that cooks our Thanksgiving turkeys. "The truth is, all the *nuclear waste* now on hand and yet to be accumulated between now and the year 2000 could be stacked on a single football field, and that stack would be only six feet high." [See FOOTBALL] 2. 1983. The subject of a national burial-site search that will be delayed until 1990. [See LEGACY]

See Notekeeping

102

Nu·cle·ar weap·ons (po͞of), n., 1967. Inventions that could have won the war in Vietnam. [See FULL TECHNOLOGICAL POWER]

Nuts ($#%&!), exclamation, 1987. Undefined. "There are some in Congress who think that they have me trapped, that this time I'll have no choice but to raise taxes or gut our defenses. *Nuts!*"

Nyet (nōp), n., 1984. [Russian] An illustration of the President's bilingual charm. After meeting with Soviet Foreign Minister Andrei Gromyko: "Now I've learned to speak Russian — *Nyet.*" [See LAUGHTER IN THE KREMLIN]

O

Oat · meal meat (kwor′ ter poun′ der), n., 1984. Fried cereal patties that the President ate during the Great Depression, without carping about the lack of government handouts.

Oc · to · ber sur · prise (dēl), n., 1980. The nightmarish possibility that the Iranian hostages would be freed prior to the 1980 election.

Off night, an (kud not täk), n., 1984. The President's first debate against Democratic candidate Walter Mondale. [Contributed by White House aides] [See UM HUMM]

Off our backs (and in our yer′ in), n., 1965–88. Where government should "get."

Ol · lie Chro · nol · o · gy (lī), n., 1986. A phony document drafted by Lieutenant Colonel Oliver *"Ollie"* North and some other White House helpers to educate the public about Iranscam and contribute to the President's plausible deniability.

See One tough son of a bitch

One plane (san′ tuhz slā′), n., 1986. An imaginary airship that could carry all the weapons America sold to Iran. [See CLARIFICATION]

One tough son of a bitch (mē!), n., 1982. Ronald Wilson Reagan.

Op · er · a · tion · al cap · a · bil · i · ty (big werd), 1981–88. Ability.

Op · er · a · tion I · vy League (dres rē her′ sl), n., 1982. A long overdue "mock nuclear war" staged within the White House. This secret, four-day exercise could turn out to be America's winning edge in World War III. [See EMERGEN-CY CHANGE-OF-ADDRESS CARDS]

Or · der · ly so · ci · e · ty, an (pō lēs′ stāt), n., 1984. Utopia.

O · rig · i · nal in · tent (hē wuz ther?), n., 1985. Our founding fathers' true goals, even if they didn't always choose the proper words when writing the Constitution. [Contributed by Attorney General Edwin Meese III]

Out · law states (fēndz), n., 1985. Libya, North Korea, Cuba, Iran and Nicaragua, which are "run by the strangest collection of misfits, looney tunes and squalid criminals since the advent of the Third Reich." [See BITBURG CEMETERY]

Out · side forc · es (kath′ lik nunz), n., 1984. Marxist demons who cause free societies to go bad. "I think they [the Nicaraguan people] are being subverted, or they're being directed by *outside forces*." [See LIBERALS]

O · ver my dead bod · y (if kon′ gres vōts it), n., 1. 1984. The only possible scenario for a tax increase. [See USERS FEES] 2. 1987. The only possible scenario for Robert H. Bork to not be confirmed to the U.S. Supreme Court.

Overreaction

O·ver·re·ac·tion (nūks), n., 1983. What the President warned to "guard against" after the Soviets shot down Korean Airlines Jet 007 and "murdered" its passengers. He stressed the need for restraint prior to a national address on television. [Contributed by White House aides] [See CRIME AGAINST HUMANITY, HORRIFYING ACT OF VIOLENCE, UNSPEAKABLE ACT, MASSACRE]

P

PACs (pox), n., 1981–88. *Political Action Committees*. These patriotic groups fund political campaigns and never ask anything in return. [See NEVER]

PAT · CO (shot doun), n., 1981. *Professional Air Traffic Controllers Organization*. A militant band of 15,000 malcontents who broke sacred federal laws and left the President no choice but to replace them. [See NEAR MISS]

Pal · ace coup (just kid′ ing), n., 1982. What it would take to cause a tax increase. [See ALEXANDER HAIG]

Pa · per (not for rēd′ ing), n., 1978. A by-product of technology that threatens future generations on this planet. "*Paper*, not nuclear waste, is our real storage problem."

Pa · per shred · der (kun fet′ ē mā′ ker), n., 1. 1983. A tool in Environmental Protection Agency Director Ann McGill

Gorsuch's heroic struggle to keep America's personal business out of the hands of Soviet dupes in Congress. 2. 1986. A tool in Lieutenant Colonel Oliver L. North's heroic struggle to keep America's personal business out of the hands of Soviet dupes in Congress. 3. 1981–88. The solution to America's real storage problem.

Par · i · ty (swap), n., 1986. The equilibrium achieved by deporting a communist spy on the same day that the Soviets release an innocent American hostage. [See DANILOFF]

Park · lane Ho · sier · y (snik′ er snik′ er), n., 1987. A store where military men go to buy nice things for little girls. [Contributed by Lieutenant Colonel Oliver L. North]

Pa · tience (wāt and wach), n., 1983. The good sportsmanship that Democrats and liberals should show while America's defense budget rises.

Peace (not tōō nīt′ mo′ mē), n., 1981–88. The plea that is whispered in the President's ear by the First Lady each night before sleep. [Contributed by the First Lady] [See HEADACHE]

Peace · keep · ers (wôr′ yorz), n., 1. 1983. Flinty-eyed U.S. Army troops sent to invade or occupy foreign countries. [See GRENADA, LEBANON] 2. 1983. A 96-ton, six-story-tall nuclear bomb that, if deployed, will lead to the day "when mankind is free of the terrible threat of nuclear weapons." [See ARMAGEDDON, MX MISSILE]

Peace move · ment (run for yor līf!), n., 1983. A worldwide campaign that will lead to war.

Peace of · fen · sive (pē ar′ stunt), n., 1981. An act of aggression in the form of an act of peace. The Soviets launched the first known "*peace offensive*," craftily recognized by the President as "a propaganda campaign to reduce missiles in Europe."

See **Peacekeeper**

Pee · wee pow · er · house (yes deer), n., 1987. The First Lady.

Pe · or · i · a (mā′ ber ē), n., 1982. The ideological capital of America. "I know what we've been doing doesn't read well in the *Washington Post* or the *New York Times*, but, believe me, it reads well in *Peoria*."

Per · jur · y (lit′ er ing), n., 1987. One of those dinky little no-no's that everybody does now and then. [See MICHAEL DEAVER, GEORGE WASHINGTON]

Per · sian Gulf (trap), n., 1987. A no-win situation. America must patrol these heavily mined waters, or else the Soviets might.

Pho · to op · por · tu · ni · ties (chēz), n., 1980–88. Evidence that the President is still alive.

Phy · sics pack · age (chān re ak′ shun), n., 1987. The detonator for a nuclear bomb. [Contributed by National Security Advisor Colin L. Powell]

Plaus · i · ble de · ni · a · bil · i · ty (dōnt tel mē), n., 1987. The White House policy of protecting the President from information that would render him responsible for White House policy. [Concocted by Rear Admiral John M. Poindexter]

Po · lit · i · cal mach · i · na · tion (wut did yōō eks pekt′), n., 1984. The Soviets' crybaby pull-out of America's Summer Olympics.

Po · lit · i · cal sav · age · ry (i want mi mā′ pō), n., 1987. Treasonous attacks by critics of Supreme Court nominee Robert H. Bork. [See GINSBURG]

Pol·y·graphs (trĭ′ el bī or dēl′), n., 1. 1983. Lie-detector tests to find out which White House aides are telling all those woppers to reporters. [See LEAKS] 2. 1985. Lie-detector tests that Secretary of State George P. Shultz refuses to take. [Contributed by Mr. Shultz]

Po·ny (brit sid), n., 1981–88. The punch line of the President's favorite anecdote: A child wakes up Christmas morning to find a pile of manure under his tree. He happily cries, "There must be a *pony!*" [See SPIN CONTROL]

Pooped (suh dā′ ted), adj., 1966. Pertaining to the crippling fatigue that strikes during media questioning. "I'm not sure I know what I'm talking about. I'm so *pooped.* You're boring in on me, aren't you? You're boring in because you know you've caught me so *pooped* that I don't know what I'm doing." [See PLAUSIBLE DENIABILITY]

Poor peo·ple (hē ne′ ver met wun), n., 1983. Actors who wear rags, pick through garbage and sleep on heating grates to embarrass the President. "I think that they have money." [Condescended by White House Counsellor Edwin Meese III]

Po·ten·tial en·ter·prise zones (up′ sīd), n., 1985. Slum neighborhoods. [See PONY]

Pre·pub·li·ca·tion re·view (sen′ ser ship), n., 1984. A reasonable check to be darn sure that none of our top 128,000 federal workers will ever go writing stuff that the Soviets could use to bring us to our knees.

Pres·i·den·tial (pub′ lik im′ ij), adj., 1984. Best. [See PHOTO OPPORTUNITY, POPE, ROSE GARDEN]

See **Prettier wives**

Press con · fer · ence (fēd′ ing sesh′ un), n., 1. 1966–80. A chance to tackle questions from reporters. 2. 1981–84. A chance to tell anecdotes to reporters. [See CLARIFICATION] 3. 1985. A fiery duel of wits with leftist handwringers. [See SAM DONALDSON] 4. 1986. A chance for White House spokesman Larry Speakes to tackle questions from reporters. 5. 1987. A chance to tackle questions from sixth graders. 6. 1987–88. [See RADIO ADDRESS]

Pret · ti · er wives (huh′ ba huh′ ba), n., 1980. One of the many advantages that Republicans have over Democrats.

Priv · a · ti · za · tion (giv′ uh wāz), n., 1985. The sale of public assets to millionaires. [See DRILLING RIGHTS]

Pro · ac · tive (shūt first), adj., 1984. Pertaining to the arrests of potential terrorists before it's too late — and they are nearly in a possible position to potentially get us. [See DOMESTIC SPYING]

Pro · com · pe · ti · tion plan (dē reg yōō lā′ shun), n., 1983. The way to cut medical costs: turn over all that health and hospital stuff to private industry. [See MAGIC OF THE MARKETPLACE, DALKON SHIELD]

Proj · ect De · moc · ra · cy (front), n., 1986. A series of fund-raising slide shows hosted by Lieutenant Colonel Oliver L. North to buy TV commercials for Freedom. [See SLUSH FUND]

Pro · pa · gan · da (wirdz), n., 1966–88. Statements by Cubans, Ethiopians, Grenadans, Iranians, Libyans, North Koreans, North Vietnamese, Palestinians, Red Chinese, Salvadorans, Sandinistas, Soviets and Democrats and liberals. [See TOTALITARIANISM]

Pro · tec · tion · ism (hed in thuh sand), n., 1979. "A bunker mentality" foreign policy that threatens "a great many American jobs [that] are dependent on the import-export trade." [See BECHTEL POWER CORP.]

Pro · tec · tive mode (kuv′ er up), n., 1987. The natural instincts of a woman to shred documents for her man. "I don't use the word 'cover-up.' I was purely in a *protective mode*." [Contributed by National Security Council personal secretary Fawn Hall]

Pro · trac · ted con · ven · tion · al war (ram′ bō for), n., 1981. The hand-to-hand combat that America had better be ready to win when Soviet-Cuban forces invade.

Psy · chol · o · gists (eg′ hedz), n., 1967. "Head-shrinkers" who work at "the biggest hotel chain in the state. (The California Department of Mental Hygiene)"

Pub · lic for · ests (for sāl), n., 1979. Federal land that "lag[s] behind well-managed private forests in productivity." [See PRIVATIZATION]

Pur · ple silk dress · es (with mach′ ing ī′ sha dō), n., 1986. Former Environmental Protection Administration Director Anne Gorsuch Burford's fatal flaw. "I would have been a lot better off if I weighed 200 pounds, looked like Ma Kettle and wore Army boots. I wore *purple silk dresses*, and I'm sure that threw them off." [Contributed by Mrs. Burford]

Q

Quest for ex·cel·lence (lām duk), n., 1987–88. The official theme of the President's final two years in office.

Ques·tions (nō nō), n., 1981–88. What White House aides painstakingly avoid asking. [Contributed by Assistant Secretary of State Elliot Abrams, National Security Council personal secretary Fawn Hall, National Security Advisor Robert McFarlane, Attorney General Edwin Meese III, National Security Council Advisor John M. Poindexter, White House Chief of Staff Donald T. Regan, Major General Richard V. Secord, Secretary of Defense Caspar W. Weinberger and Vice President George H. W. Bush]

Quiche and cha·blis move·ment (yup′ ēz), n., 1982. [French] The nuclear freeze campaign. [See FOREIGN AGENTS]

See **Radio address**

R

Rad·i·o ad·dress (gud dā′!), n., 1982–87. A weekly show
hosted by the President that follows Paul Harvey News.

Ram·bo (rok′ ē), n., 1985. A film that depicted options for
combating communism. It gave the President an idea for
"what to do next time this [terrorism] happens." [See AIR
STRIKE]

Ran·som (dēl), n., 1986. Something America will never pay.
[See NEVER]

Read·ers Di·gest (hyo͞o′ mer in yo͞o′ ni form), n., 1982. A
technical manual studied by the President for scraps of information about Soviet infiltration of the nuclear freeze
campaign.

Rea·gan Doc·trine, The (a gresh′ un), n., 1985. The policy of
doing unto other countries what the CIA says to do. [See
ONE TOUGH SON OF A BITCH]

119

Rea·gan, Nan·cy Dav·is (mä′ mē), n., 192?– . 1. Wife and mother. 2. 1981–86. White House Chief of Staff. 3. 1986–87. The forty-first President of the United States.

Rea·gan·auts (kemps), n., 1981. Disciples.

Rea·gan·om·ics (stock′ man blōō it), n., 1981. [Also Supply side economics, Voodoo economics] The strategy of cutting taxes while doubling the federal deficit. [See ARMAGEDDON]

Rea·gan, Ron·ald (rä′ nē), n., 1911– . 1. 1920. "Dutch," a young lad growing up in Dixon, Illinois. 2. 1932. A graduate of Eureka College, near Peoria, Illinois. [See PEORIA] 3. 1933. The radio voice of the University of Iowa Hawkeyes football team. [See SPIN CONTROL] 4. 1937–65. Actor. [See GIRLS ON PROBATION, JUKE GIRL, NAUGHTY BUT NICE] 5. 1940. Actor who played "The Gipper." [See KNUTE ROCKNE, ALL-AMERICAN] 6. 1943–49. Informant for the Federal Bureau of Investigation. [See DOMESTIC SPYING] 7. 1947–53. President of the Screen Actors' Guild. [See PATCO] 8. 1947. "Friendly" witness before the U.S. House Committee on Un-American Activities [See BLACKLIST] 9. 1954–62. Host of "General Electric Theater" TV series. [See DEFENSE CONTRACTS] 10. 1962–64. Host of "Death Valley Days" TV series. [See BORAXO] 11. 1966–75. Governor of California. [See BOTULISM] 12. 1976–80. Newspaper columnist and radio commentator. [See PAUL HARVEY] 13. 1981–88. President of the United States. [See DR. STRANGELOVE] 14. 1982. What people should "let Reagan be." [Contributed by Secretary of the Interior James G. Watt] 15. 1983. "One tough son of a bitch." [See GRENADA, HELLCATS OF THE NAVY] 16. 1984. "The Gipper." [See KNUTE ROCKNE, ALL-AMERICAN] 17. 1985. A freedom fighter. "I'm a Contra too." [See RAMBO] 18. 1986–88. "Dutch," a young lad growing up in Dixon, Illinois.

Re · al Is · sue, the (smōk skrēn), n., 1984. Whether American children should pray in public schools. [See CONGRESS]

Re · al · ists (krā′ zēz), n., 1982. Men in the White House who plan America's post-World War III policies. [Contributed by White House aides] [See ORDERLY SOCIETY]

Real · ly min · us · cule (ēn′ sē wēn′ sē), adj., 1986. Pertaining to a ninety-ton shipment of arms to Iran.

Re · birth of pa · tri · o · tism (ya hōō′), n., 1987. The President's greatest achievement: transforming American youth from a bunch of bums who were "demonstrating about all sorts of things" to responsible citizens who are "waiting in line to enlist." [See ARLINGTON CEMETERY, RAMBO]

Re · ces · sion (dē presh′ un), n., 1. 1981–82. A soggy economy caused by former President Jimmy Carter. 2. 1988–89. A soggy economy caused by former President Jimmy Carter.

Red tide, the (red dawn), n., 1985. The wave of humanity that will pour into America when Nicaraguan tanks roll across Mexico.

Re · flag · ging of tank · ers (es kū lā′ shun), n., 1987. The sudden blooming of America's stars-and-stripes pride in Middle Eastern waters. [See MINES]

Re · form · ist gov · ern · ment (dik′ tā ter), n., 1985. The kindly administration of Pieter W. Botha in South Africa. [See ORDERLY SOCIETY]

Reg · u · la · to · ry re · lief (nō rōōlz), n., 1981. The elimination of federal laws requiring businesses to act ethically.

See **Rescue mission**

Re·port·ers (haks), n., 1981–88. Handwringers and merchants of misery who, if allowed to tag along on rescue missions, would get in the way of the news that Americans want to hear.

Re·pub·li·cans (wīt hats), n., 1982. Americans. [Contributed by Secretary of the Interior James G. Watt]

Res·cue mis·sion (wôr), n., 1. 1983. The invasion of a small country to save it from communism. [See NOT ONE SQUARE INCH] 2. 1984. A place where rich people dine for free. [Contributed by Attorney General Edwin Meese III] [See SOUP KITCHEN]

Re·spon·si·bil·i·ty (ha ha′), n., 1. 1982. Accountability accepted, belatedly, for the attempt to exempt Bob Jones University from taxes. "The truth is out... No one put anything over on me... I'm the originator of the whole thing." 2. 1987. Accountability accepted, briefly, for the funneling of private money to the Contras. "I've known what's going on here, as a matter of fact, for quite a long time now, a matter of years... [It] was my idea to begin with." [See MEMORY]

Rev·en·ue en·hance·ment (kwik buks), n., 1984. A tax. [See PALACE COUP]

Re·verse dis·crim·i·na·tion (em ploi′ ing blaks), n., 1984. The reason Republicans don't always get hired.

Re·vi·sion·ism (for get′ thuh past), n., 1987–88. The art of re-remembering how great everything was back when Richard Nixon was president.

Ri·ot·ing (wutz thuh prob′lem?), n., 1985. The reason for unrest in South Africa.

Rock 'n' roll (bun′ ē hop), n., 1987. The music of the Presidency. "Some said that I was singing golden oldies, nothing new. Well, the line item veto and the balanced budget amendment may be oldies but they're goodies. And those who think they don't stand a chance on the charts had better keep their dial tuned to this station. It's *rock 'n' roll* time again in the White House." [See WAYNE NEWTON]

Ron San (mē), n., 1983. [Japanese] The President. [Contributed by Japanese Prime Minister Yasuhiro Nakasone] "And he calls me Yasu." [See MON CHER RON]

Roy · al · ly P. · O.'d (uh wāk′), adj., 1987. Presidentially angry. [Contributed by National GOP Co-Chairman Maureen Reagan] [See LEADING THE WAY]

Rug mer · chants (for′ in erz), n., 1987. Iranians. [Contributed by former White House Chief of Staff Donald T. Regan]

Rus · sian mech · an · ics (oops), n., 1987. Rock-ribbed Soviet masters of technology. "Send them to Detroit, because we could use that kind of ability." [Contributed by Vice President George H. W. Bush] [See DEEP DOO-DOO]

See **Rock 'n' roll**

S

SALT (salt), n., 1. 1981. *S*trategic *A*rms *L*imitation *T*alks, a sellout treaty that threatened the world with arms control. 2. 1983. Sodium chloride, used sparingly at the White House for health reasons. "You'd have to be a raccoon or something to eat a hard-boiled egg without *salt*. But I use very little."

S·D·I (star wôrz), n., 1985–86. *S*trategic *D*efense *I*nitiative. A computerized peace umbrella with ray guns, secret codes and spaceships that must be deployed before it is designed, because that's what the Soviets are doing. [See B-1 BOMBER, FLYING EDSEL]

START (stäl), n., 1. 1981. *S*trategic *A*rms *R*eduction *T*alks, of which "nothing will have a higher priority." 2. 1982–88. [See MEMORY]

Sales·man (wil′ ē lō′ mun), n., 1984. The President's job. While

127

visiting China: "Doing everything I can up to the point of putting a 'Buy America' sticker on my bag." [See Working Vacation, Everthing We Can]

San·din·i·stas (bad gīz), n., 1986. Spanish-speaking communist "monsters" who dress up like freedom fighters and kill innocent people just to give the Contras a bad name. [See Parklane Hosiery]

Screw·driver (bar′ gin), n., 1983. A tool purchased by the U.S. Navy from General Electric Co. for $780. [See Toilet Seat Cover]

Sec·ond A·mer·i·can Rev·o·lu·tion (werz pak′ wud?), n., 1985. An easy-to-understand tax reform package. [See Migraine]

Se·cret dip·lo·mat·ic in·i·ti·a·tive (dōnt tel kon′ gres), n., 1986. The swap of 300 TOWs for an AMCIT. [See Amcit]

Sed·a·tion (kōk and as′ per in), n., 1986. A drug-induced state in which a president is liable to do anything, even swing deals with terrorists. [Conjured by Attorney General Edwin Meese III] [See Chemical People]

Se·nil·i·ty (charj, men!), n., 1980. Mental deterioration into a childlike state, commonly associated with old age. Feelings of "*senility*" would prompt the President to immediately resign from office. [See Cowboys, Mommy, Nap, Pony]

Set-a·sides (pā′ bak), n., 1986. Federal contracts guaranteed to white businessmen who hire minority or women figureheads. [See Actors]

Sep·ar·a·tion of church and state (Yeah, rīt), n., 1988. The "fundamental value" that flashed before George H. W.

See **Shredding party**

Bush's eyes when the Japs shot down his plane during WWII. [Concocted by Vice President Bush]

Sharks (sam don′ uld sun), n., 1986. The bloodthirsty American press.

Shin · ing cit · y on a hill (tuh lē′ dō), n., 1976. The glowing utopia America could be, if not for Democrats and liberals. [See RADIOACTIVITY]

Shov · el (sĭ′ un ĭd kap′ sl), n., 1982. The key to surviving nuclear war. "Dig a hole. Cover it with a couple of doors. And then throw three feet of dirt on top. Everyone's going to make it if there are enough *shovels* to go around." [Contributed by Deputy Under Secretary of Defense Thomas K. Jones] [See EMERGENCY CHANGE-OF-ADDRESS CARDS]

Shov · el bri · gade (ank il dēp′), n., 1. 1986. A team of White House aides who explain policy to the press. [Contributed by White House Chief of Staff Donald T. Regan] 2. 1982–88. [See SHOVEL]

Shred · ding par · ty (shredz ma ken′ zē), n., 1986. A get-together during which Lieutenant Colonel Oliver L. North, his personal secretary and a few good eggs from the Justice Department tackle those legendary mounds of federal paperwork. [See BELLY BUTTON]

Shut up (shhh), v., 1. 1980. To request silence of hecklers. "Aww, *shut up!*" 2. 1982. To request silence of Republicans. "*Shut up!*" 3. 1983. To request silence of Congress. "Put up or *shut up!*" 4. 1987. To offer Presidential silence. "You won't be able to *shut* me *up* (after the Iran-Contra hearings)."

Sic 'em (sel thuh rītz), v., 1981. The President's instructions to Secretary of the Interior James G. Watt before sending him out to protect America's environment. [Contributed by Mr. Watt]

Silk · worm mis · siles (dir′tē bomz), n., 1987. Modern weaponry that should never have been allowed to fall into the hands of Iranian madmen. [See ARMS TRANSFERS]

Slav · er · y (wirk), n., 1962. What the Soviets have in mind for America. "We can lose our freedom all at once by succumbing to Russian aggression, or we can lose it gradually by installments. The end result is *slavery*." [See INTERNAL REVENUE SERVICE]

Sleaze fac · tor (hōō us?), n., 1981–87. A trumped-up political issue raised by Democrats and liberals merely because a few Presidential appointees resigned or were probed for something or other. [See RICHARD V. ALLEN, JAMES BEGGS, CARLOS CAMPBELL, WILLIAM J. CASEY, MICHAEL K. DEAVER, CAROL DINKINS, ELIZABETH HANFORD DOLE, RAY DONOVAN, JOHN FEDDERS, GUY FISKE, JAYNE GALLAGHER, ANNE GORSUCH BURFORD, ARTHUR HAYES, J. LYNN HELMS, JOHN W. HERNANDEZ, ROBERT HILL, JOHN HORTON, MAX HUGEL, RITA LAVELLE, ROBERT C. MCFARLANE, MARJORIE MECKLENBERG, EDWIN MEESE III, JONATHAN MILLER, RICHARD R. MILLER, ROBERT NIMMO, FRANKLIN C. "LYN" NOFZIGER, OLIVER L. NORTH, MATTHEW NOVICK, THEODORE OLSEN, CLARENCE M. PENDLETON, JR., ROBERT PERRY, J. WILLIAM PETRO, JOHN M. POINDEXTER, THOMAS C. REED, DONALD T. REGAN, EMMANUEL SAVAS, EDMUND SCHMULTS, RICHARD V. SECORD, VICTOR SCHROEDER, VICTOR THOMPSON, JOHN TODHUNTER, PETER VOSS, JAMES G. WATT, CHARLES Z. WICK]

Slush fund (big buks), n., 1986. A $90-million component of America's defense budget.

Smok · ing gun (pro͞of), n., 1987. A Presidential memo about Iranscam that was not shredded by Lieutenant Colonel Oliver L. North, because it does not exist. "There ain't no *smoking gun.*"

So · cial is · sues (ginz′ bergz tar′ gets), n., 1981–88. Abortion, the death penalty, busing and school prayer.

So · cial jus · tice (kops), n., 1981. What American troops would bring to El Salvador. [See COLLATERAL DAMAGE]

So · cial re · forms (spend′ ing), n., 1978. Do-gooder programs that "rob us of that great sense of generosity and charity that is our American heritage."

So · cial safe · ty net (nuh′ thing), n., 1981. A collection of programs that offer delicious food, fine clothing and warm shelter to Americans lucky enough to qualify. [See SOUP KITCHENS]

So · cial se · cu · ri · ty (wāst), n., 1. 1964–79. "A welfare program" that should be gutted. 2. 1980. A pay-back program that will be maintained. 3. 1981–83. A welfare program that should be gutted. 4. 1984. A pay-back program that will be maintained. 5. 1985–88. A welfare program that should be gutted.

So · cial se · cu · ri · ty re · form (wanna bī a brij?), n., 1981. A 20 percent reduction of government handouts to the elderly. [See DOGFOOD]

So·ci·ol·o·gy ma·jors (ther′ gud mar′ shul), n., 1986. Liberal judges who removed prayer from classrooms and caused America's drug epidemic. [See GINSBURG]

Sog·gy e·con·o·my (rē sesh′ un), n., 1982. A 10.8 percent unemployment rate during the President's administration. [See DEPRESSION]

Soup Kitch·en (fôr′ star res′ ta ront), n., 1984. A place where rich people dine for free. [Contributed by Attorney General Edwin Meese III] [See RESCUE MISSION]

South Af·ri·ca (a par′ tīd), n., 1985. An American ally that has "eliminated the segregation that we once had in our own country — the type of thing where hotels and restaurants and places of entertainment and so forth were segregated — that has all been eliminated." [See REFORMIST GOVERNMENT]

South Suc·co·tash (thuh north ēst′), n., 1982. A place where plant closings should not be reported. "Is it news that some fellow in *South Succotash* someplace has just been laid off, that he should be interviewed nationwide?" [See UNION OF SOVIET SOCIALIST REPUBLICS]

Spe·cial in·ter·ests (op ō zi′ shun), n., 1984. Labor unions.

Spin con·trol (sā en′ ē thing), n., 1985. The practice of occasionally reminding leftist reporters that folks across this great land are darn tired of hearing bad things said about America. [See PONY]

Spir·it·u·al ex·haus·tion (burn′ out), n., 1981. What the Soviet Union suffers from. [Contributationalized by Secretary of State Alexander M. Haig, Jr.]

Spir·it·u·al re·a·wak·en·ing (chirch ē′ kwilz stāt), n., 1984. The renewed bond between God and America due to the President's hard work. "Church attendance is up. Audiences for religious books and broadcasts are growing." [See JIM AND TAMMY BAKKER, JERRY FALWELL, ORAL ROBERTS, PAT ROBERTSON]

Split the dif·fer·ence (rōl thuh dīs), v., 1982. The only fair way to settle complex budget controversies between cabinet officials.

Spot ads (bor ak′ sō), n., 1987. Television commericals for Freedom that Lieutenant Colonel Oliver L. North said he will buy with money raised from private donors. [See LYING]

Spy dust (ah chōō′), n., 1985. A diabolical tool of Soviet duplicity. Special lint is sprayed on Americans, and they are tracked throughout Moscow. [See LAUGHTER IN THE KREMLIN]

Squeal rule (no pri′ vuh sē), n., 1983. A phrase from the leftist press that tries to smear the long overdue federal requirement that doctors merely call up young people's parents before filling them full of satanic garbage about birth control. [See AIDS, CONDOMS]

Stand·ing tall (grr), adj., 1984. America's erect feeling after the rescue mission in Grenada.

Star Wars (es dē ī), n., 1. 1981. A great American film in which Freedom defeats Communism in outer space. 2. 1985. A really unscientific way to describe America's outer space peace umbrella.

Stealth (shh), n., 1980. A famous aircraft that the Soviets don't know about.

Sub·min·i·mum wage (tū ten per our), n., A boost to the economy that, if supported by Democrats and liberals, would allow more fast food restaurants to hire more senior citizens.

Sup·ply side e·con·om·ics (num′ berz), n., 1981. The simple fact that if you cut taxes and raise defense spending, everything will turn out all right. [See DEFICIT]

Sur·ren·der or die (nūk′ um), n., 1985. What the Soviets will tell America if they think they can beat us in a war. [See UNCLE]

Sur·veil·lance (wīr′ taps), n., 1986. The key to identifying drug addicts. "*Surveillance* of problem areas such as locker rooms, parking lots, shipping and mailroom areas and nearby taverns, if necessary." [Contributed by Attorney General Edwin Meese III]

Sur·viv·a·bil·i·ty (chōōz hōō livz), n., 1980. What America must achieve to bring home the bacon in World War III. "You have a *survivability* of command and control, *survivability* of industrial potential, protection of a percentage of your citizens. . .that's the way you can have a winner." [Contributed by Vice President George H. W. Bush] [See SHOVEL]

Swiss bank ac·count (taks shel′ ter), n., 1986. [Swiss] A storage facility for research and development funds in the war against totalitarianism. [See SLUSH FUND]

Sym·met·ry (eks kyōōs′), n., 1984. The doctrine that says America has a right to invade Nicaragua because the Soviets are in El Salvador.

T

Tac · ti · cal pes · si · mism (luks baaaad), n., 1985. The art of
composing gloomy forecasts for arms control talks, so that
whatever happens looks hopeful by comparison. [Con-
tributed by White House aides] [See SPIN CONTROL]

Tax in · crease (yōō′ zerz fē), n., 1984. Something that will never
happen, "nor will I allow any plans" for one. [See NEVER]

Tax re · form (hīk), n., 1986. A plan to generate more federal income without raising taxes. [See USERS FEES]

Tech · niques of per · sua · sion (ter′ or izm), n., 1984. The CIA's
strategy to win the hearts of Central Americans, as outlined
in a booklet distributed to freedom fighters. Among the
techniques are teaching peasants to read, harvesting crops
and killing public officials. [Contributed by CIA Director
William J. Casey]

Tech · nol · o · gy (brand nōō gunz), n., 1978. The answer.

Tef · lon (wēk pres), n., 1981–86. An invisible shield against demagoguery and character assassination brandished by an advocate of God in the crusade against totalitarianism.

Tel · e · Promp · ter (id' ē ut kardz), n., 1981–88. A machine the President gazes into when speaking from the heart.

Tem · po · rar · y dis · lo · ca · tions (pink slips), n., 1982. Layoffs.

Ter · ror · ists (dem' ō krats), n., 1985. Barbarians who try to get their way through violence against innocent people. If "you just aim in the general direction and kill some people, well, then you're a *terrorist* too." [See COLLATERAL DAMAGE]

Test · ing (thawt kun trol'), n., 1. 1985. The way to learn who is speaking to reporters. [See POLYGRAPHS] 2. 1986. The way to learn who takes illegal drugs. [See URINE] 3. 1987. The way to learn who has AIDS. [See MARRIAGE] 4. 1966–88. Governmental intrusion into the rights of private companies as they try to develop new life-saving drugs. [See NUTRASWEET]

There you go a · gain (bro' ken rek' erd), exclamation, 1. 1980. A great debate one-liner that clarifies the President's stance on Social Security and really puts Democrats where they belong — on the griddle. 2. 1984. A throwaway line that Democrats and a few smart-aleck reporters are raising heck about because of the President's stance on Social Security. [See SOCIAL SECURITY]

Thin blue line, the (big bruh' ther), n., 1981. The police barrier that "holds back a jungle which threatens to reclaim this clearing we call civilization." [See JUNGLE]

Third floor (hel′hōl), n., 1981. A disgraceful White House netherworld that has been reclaimed by the First Lady. "Nothing had been done on the *third floor* in thirty years. There were cracks in the walls. It needed painting. It needed maintaining." [Contributed by the First Lady]

Thor · ough · bred per · form · ance (ä′ther ä′ther), n., 1980. A description of the President's debating victory over Democrat Jimmy Carter, as announced by ABC Newsman George Will. [Contributed by Reagan debate coach George Will]

Throw-weights (jar′gun), n., 1985. Definition unattempted: considered too complex for female readers. They "are not going to understand *throw-weights* or what is happening in Afghanistan or what is happening in human rights." [Contributed by White House Chief of Staff Donald T. Regan] [See GENDER GAP]

Time · ly fash · ion (dōnt hōld yer breth), n., 1986. The speed at which the President should notify the Congress of deals with terrorists and of secret wars. [See COLD DAY IN HADES]

Tiny lit · tle gun (dī skum), n., 1981. The First Lady's personal firearm. [See BITE THE BULLET]

Toi · let seat cov · er (kä′mart), n., 1985. A $640 expenditure for the U.S. Air Force. [See SCREWDRIVER]

To · tal · i · tar · i · an · ism (no͞o dēl), n., 1984. The inevitable consequence of Democrat and liberal policies: "More government authority, less individual liberty, and ultimately, *totalitarianism*." [See CLEAN WATER ACT]

Tow · er Com · mis · sion (färs), n., 1986. A government tribunal that concluded that the President sleeps a little too much.

See **Tree**

Trade def·i·cit (owt of kun trōl'), n., 1988. "A sign of strength."

Tra·di·tion·al fam·i·ly (hī huh' nē, werz bē' ver?) The natural structure of human relations: hubby works, and mom cleans house. [Contributed by White House Communications Director Patrick J. Buchanan] [See LITTLE HOUSE ON THE PRAIRIE]

Tra·di·tion·al val·ues (a' pul pī), n., 1980. "Family, work, neighborhood, freedom, peace." [See NINETEEN-EIGHTY -FOUR]

Train·ers (trōōps), n., 1983. American soldiers in El Salvador.

Tree (wēd), n., 1. 1966. No big deal. "I mean, if you've looked at a hundred thousand acres or so, of *trees*, you know, a *tree* is a *tree*, how many more do you need to look at?" 2. 1979. A major threat to the environment. "Eighty percent of air pollution comes not from chimneys and auto exhaust pipes, but from plants and *trees*." [See PAPER]

Trick·cle down the·o·ry (did thā bī it?), n., 1981. The proven fact that financial aid for the rich will help poor people, eventually. [See CLARIFICATION]

Tru·ly need·y (ded), n., 1982. People who are not merely needy and, thus, deserve help. [Say CHEESE]

Two-term lim·it (thank god), n., 1987. An example of government overregulation that robs Americans of the right to re-elect the President forever.

Two-track (kā' äs), adj., 1982. The art of installing missiles in Europe while negotiating to reduce missiles in Europe. [See EUROPE]

See Uncle

U

Uh huh (yawn), exclamation, 1987. The President's reponse to
urgings by National GOP Co-chairman Maureen Reagan
to fire Iranscam conspirators. [Contributed by Chairman
Reagan]

Ul · ti · mate co · vert op · er · a · tion (sē′ krit wôrz), n., 1986. The
pinnacle of America's espionage professionals: secretly selling arms to bad guys to fund the actions of good guys. [Con-
tributed by CIA Director William J. Casey]

Um humm (help), n., 1984. The President's fiery comeback to
this debate question from democratic candidate Walter
Mondale: "Mr. President, you said, 'There you go again,'
right? Remember the last time you said that?" [See SOCIAL
SECURITY, MEMORY]

Un · cle (yo͞o win), n., 1985. An exclamation that, if uttered
sincerely by Nicaraguan president Daniel Ortega, would

eliminate the need for U.S. military involvement in Central America. "If they'd say, '*Uncle*'. All right, come on back into the revolutionary government, and let's straighten this out." [See MAKE MY DAY]

Un · de · sir · a · bles (pôr pē′ pul), n., 1967. What a raise in tuition at the University of California would "help us get rid of."

Un · em · ploy · ment in · sur · ance (wel′ fer), n., 1966. "A prepaid vacation for a segment of our society which has made it a way of life." [See LAYOFFS]

Un · ion of So · viet So · cial · ist Re · pub · lics (rush′ uh), n., 1982. The Evil Empire. "There is sin and evil in the world. And we are enjoined by scripture to oppose it with all our might . . . Let us pray for the salvation of those who live in that totalitarian darkness — pray that they will discover the joy of knowing God. But until they do, let us be aware that they are the focus of evil in the modern world." [See TED KENNEDY, USEFUL IDIOT FOR KREMLIN PROPAGANDA]

Un · ions (tēm′ sterz), n., 1. 1981. Steadfast enemies of communist tyranny in Poland, whose courage lights a beacon for workers everywhere. 2. 1981. Spoiled, insubordinate enemies of authority, without whom we can control our air traffic just as well. [See PATCO]

Un · nec · es · sar · y ob · sta · cles (in spek′ shunz), n., 1981. Safety regulations that are delaying the construction of badly needed nuclear power plants. [See NUCLEAR WARNING SHOT]

Up · ping the peace an · te (es kuh lā′ shun), v., 1988. Requesting more money for freedom fighters in Nicaragua. [Contributed by *USA Today*]

U · rine (pē), n., 1986. A truth serum in the war on crack. The President holds no fear of the results of his *urine* test "because I know what I put in." [See LEADING THE WAY, SEDATION]

Use · ful id · i · ot for Krem · lin prop · a · gan · da (hōō mē?), n., 1987. An American president who, by caving in to a nagging wife, relaxes his trigger finger on the God-given nuclear arsenals that preserve freedom and democracy. [Contributed by National Conservative Caucus chief Howard Phillips]

Us · ers' fee (taks), n., 1982. A five-cent payment to the government — as opposed to a tax — on each gallon of gasoline sold.

U · su · al sev · en · ty-five-year-olds, the (līk rā′ gun), n., 1986. Anticommunists who donated $7.1 million to Carl R. Channel's National Endowment for the Preservation of Freedom. [Confessed by Mr. Channel]

See **Voice of reason**

V

Va·ca·tions (hôrs′ rīdz), n., 1981–88. Grueling, nose-to-the-grindstone work marathons that, each few weeks, challenge the outer limits of human endurance. These merciless sessions require "a change of scenery" from the spend-spend fantasy world of Washington. [See BARBADOS]

Ver·i·fi·ca·tion (sē for yor self′), n., 1. 1984–88. Making sure the Soviets don't cheat on an arms control treaty. 2. 1986. Making sure federal workers don't cheat on their urine tests. [See DIRECT OBSERVATION]

Ver·y fav·or·a·ble con·sid·er·a·tion (pref′ er ens), n., 1987. The justice that should be dealt to a Tennessee congressman's fine son, who just happened to be convicted of tax fraud. [Contributed by Mrs. Edwin Meese III]

Vid·e·o games (star wôrz), n., 1983. The real story! "The total amount requested for aid to all of Central America is about $600 million; that is less than one-tenth of what Americans will spend this year on coin-operated *video games*."

Vi·et·nam syn·drome (drooōōp), n., 1974–83. A feeling of impotence that once kept America from entering small countries. [See SOFT ON COMMUNISM]

Vi·et·nam War (gud old dāz), n., 1959–74. A "noble cause" in Southeast Asia that Democrats were "afraid to win." "We should declare war on North *Vietnam*. We could pave the whole country and put parking stripes on it, and still be home for Christmas." [1966]

Voice of rea·son (krook), n., 1973. President Richard Milhouse Nixon.

Vol·un·teer·ism (frē lā′bur), n., 1981. The answer. [See SOGGY ECONOMY]

Voo·doo e·con·o·mics (ī nev′er sed that), n., 1980. The President's economic policies. [Contributed by Presidential candidate George H. W. Bush]

Vot·ing with their feet (get lost), n., 1982. A strategy for economic recovery whereby jobless Northerners just move South.

W

Wal · ters, Bar · bar · a ("bē kind tōō us, mis ter prez′ u dent"), n., 1891–1988. A hard-hitting journalist and dependable messenger between Iranian arms merchant Manucher Ghorbanifar and the President. [See HUGH DOWNS]

War Pow · ers Act (not en forsd′), n., 1987. Needless government regulations on war.

Wash · ing · ton Post (nōōz), n., 1. 1982. A newspaper whose classified ads are a barometer of the economy. 2. 1982. A newspaper that does not sell in Peoria, Illinois. 3. 1986. A newspaper that prints lies. 4. 1986. A newspaper from which the President finds out what happened about Iranscam.

Waste, fraud, and a · buse (li′ unz and tī′ gerz and berz), n., 1980. The three facets of American government.

See **Watt**

Watch, my (lītz out), n., 1987. An eight-year shift as White House security guard. "As personally distasteful as I find secret bank accounts and diverted funds, well, as the Navy would say, this happened on *my watch.*" [See NAP]

Wa·ter·gate (nik′ sunz mes), n., 1975. A campaign prank that was mercilessly trumped up by Democrats and liberals. "The Republican party has traditionally been the victim of shenanigans worse than *Watergate.*" [See J. EDGAR HOOVER]

Wa·ter·gate con·spir·a·tors (wīt hous staf), n., 1973. Pranksters who "are not criminals at heart." [See BREAK-IN]

Watt, James G. (bal′ dē), n., 1981–83. A charismatic environmental evangelist whose accomplishments include the commercial development of wilderness that wasn't paying its way and numerous verbal victories over Democrats and liberals: "Every time I increase that hatred of those who oppose me, those on the other side who support me are even more willing to lay down their lives." [Contributed by Mr. Watt] [See CRIPPLE]

Wed·tech (skan′ dl), n., 1981–88. A New York City firm that would never try to bribe elected officials. [See INDICTMENT]

Wel·fare (lug′ sher ē), n., 1966. A monstrous system that "encourage[s] divorce and immorality" by trading "our freedom for the soup kitchen." [See SOUP KITCHEN]

Wel·fare queen (momz), n., 1980. A she-demon who cheats the American taxpayers out of hundreds of hard-earned dollars.

Well·der·ly (ron′ n nan′ sē), n., 1981. America's senior

See **Wimp factor**

citizens, who live in nice houses and do not want. [See Dogfood]

What do I have to say? (sā nuh' thing), exclamation, 1981–88. The President's usual question in White House policy briefings. [Contributed by White House aides] [See What We Had to Do]

What's up (ginz' bergz hed), n., 1987. What "the American people will know" if the U.S. Senate doesn't quickly confirm Douglas H. Ginsburg to the Supreme Court.

What we had to do (huh?), n., 1981–88. What we did. [See Collateral Damage]

Wheat (farm prof' itz), n., 1. 1975. A foodstuff America should never sell to Soviets. "Let their system collapse, but meantime, buy our farmers' *wheat* ourselves and have it on hand to feed the Russian people when they finally become free." [See Never] 2. 1981–88. A foodstuff America must sell to Soviets. "I've said many times our philosophy is against the unfair and wrong-headed policies of grain embargos." [1984]

Where's the Rest of Me? (gud kwes' chun), exclamation, 1. 1942. The most heartfelt line ever delivered in American cinema. In *King's Row*, the President brought moviegoers to their knees by portraying Drake McHugh, a rake whose legs have been amputated. For the wake-up scene, he convinced himself his own limbs were gone. "If I divorce myself and say, 'How does Drake McHugh feel?' it's not a good job. But if I scream in horror, '*Where's the rest of me?*' and I feel it, that's me, and it's right." 2. 1965. The title of the President's autobiography.

Whis·tle-blow·ers (lēks), n., 1981. Big mouths who, for treasonous reasons, ignore everything good about America when they run whimpering to the leftist press.

White House base · ment (ol′ ēz of′ is), n., 1986. The command center for American foreign policy.

White House mole (kā′ sē), n., 1980. An unknown brave American who liberated President Jimmy Carter's briefing book so that the Real President could win the big debate and turn this country around. [See THOROUGHBRED PERFORMANCE]

Whomp 'em (ya hōō), exclamation, 1984. To crush Democrats and liberals. "You don't just score victories. You whomp 'em." [See KICK A LITTLE ASS]

Wimp fac · tor (pan′ tē wāst), n., 1. 1983–84. The critical issue of whether Vice President Walter Mondale has any guts. [See TAX INCREASE] 2. 1987–88. An issue that if raised to Vice President George H. W. Bush means somebody is cruising for a knuckle sandwich. [See DEEP DOO-DOO]

Win · dow of op · por · tu · ni · ty (chek this out), n., 1984. An international showcase of America's mighty missiles, standing tall. [See GOSH]

Win · dow of vul · ner · a · bil · i · ty (mis′ l gap), n., 1982. A global peephole through which the Soviets can size up America's personal nuclear impotence. [See WINDOW OF OPPORTUNITY]

Wing · man (tō′ dē), n., 1986. A vice president who is loyal to his master, for better or worse. "When the flak gets heavy, the *wingman* doesn't go peeling off." [Contributed by Vice President George H. W. Bush] [See MISTAKES WERE MADE]

Wo · men (wīvz), n., 1. 1978. Flawed but basically nice people. "In spite of all the jokes men like to tell about *women* drivers, I think almost all men know in their hearts that

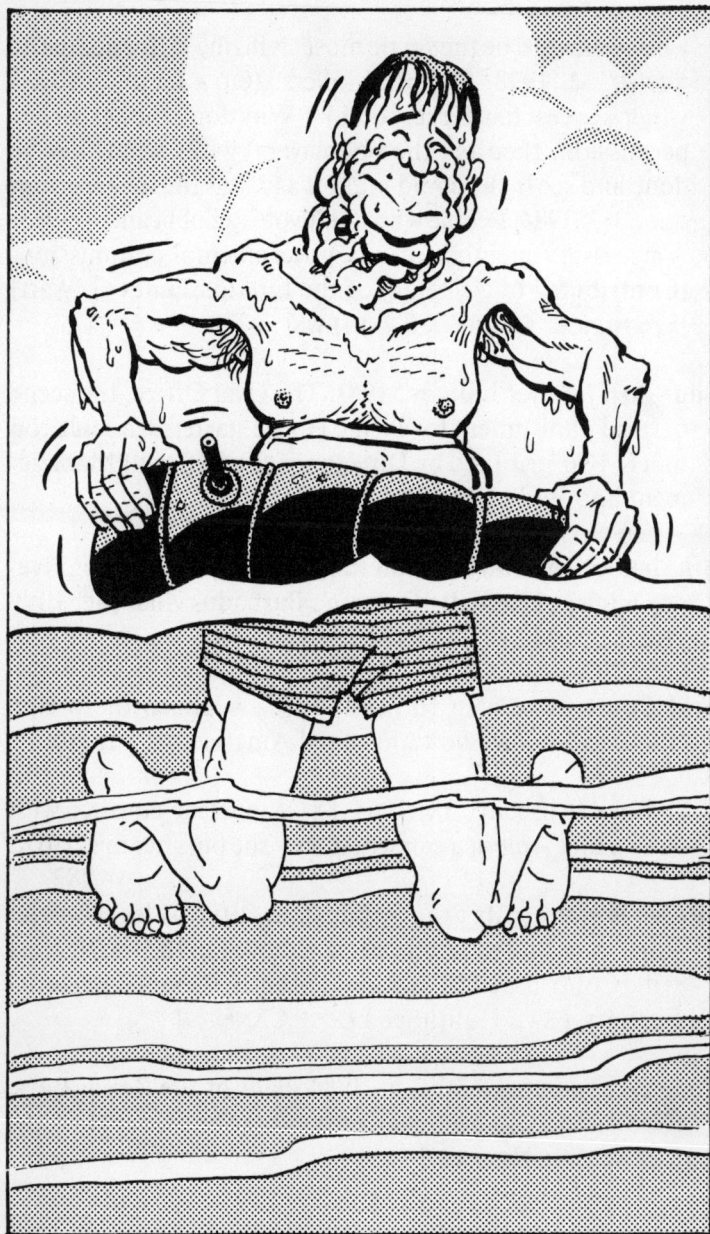

See **Working vacation**

women have to be the single most civilizing influence in the world." 2. 1978. Potential killers. (Of a female sportswriter's access to a locker room): "Why don't they grant her permission, then tell the ballplayers' wives what they've done and see if she could make it as far as the locker-room door." 3. 1984. People who don't vote Republican. 4. 1983. A necessary member of any governmental commission. [Contributed by Secretary of the Interior James G. Watt] [See BLACK, CRIPPLE, TWO JEWS]

Wood · shed (tan yer hīd′), n., 1981. The Oval Office, the scene of lurid punishment for White House staffers who talk too much. [Contributed by Director of the Office of Management and Budget David A. Stockman]

Work · ing va · ca · tion (fun fun fun), n., 1982. A grueling five-day hitch at Claudette Colbert's Barbados villa. [See BITE THE BULLET]

World Court (tē vē gām shō), n., 1985. A bunch of foreign lawyers who have no right to tell America what to do.

World War III (bōōm), n., 1965–88. A nuclear conflict with Russia that America can win if only she puts her mind to it.

Writ · ten law, the (rūlz ar for wimps), n., 1987. A legal barrier Americans must sometimes "go above" in the war against evil. [Contributed by National Security Council personal secretary Fawn Hall] [See LOOSE CANNON]

Wrong el · e · ments (yōōth), n., 1984. Fans of the Beach Boys. [Contributed by Secretary of the Interior James G. Watt] [See WAYNE NEWTON]

X, Y, Z

You ain't seen no · thin' yet (wu pē′), n., 1984. The President's promise of continued joy for America. [See AIR STRIKE, BORK, IRANSCAM, NICARAGUA, PERSIAN GULF, REFLAGGING, RECESSION, GEORGE BUSH]

Yup · pies (bā′ bē boōm′ erz), n., 1984–88. People who, considering the money they make, ought to be a little more grateful to the Republican party.

Ze · ro (tū hun′ dred and twen′ tē bil′ yun), n., 1. 1980. What the federal budget deficit will be in 1983 thanks to the President's programs. 2. 1986. What the federal budget deficit will be in 1991 thanks to the President's programs.

Ze · ro op · tion (wanna bī uh duk?), n., 1982. The President's offer to scrap 572 missiles if the Soviets would scrap 1,000.

Zzzz (so it gōz), exclamation, 1980–88. A thoughtful sound occasionally made by the President.

X,Y,Z